BECOME A PROVIDER

DISCOVER THE JOY OF BLESSING AND PROTECTING OTHERS

JUSTIN THOMAS

CL THOMAS FELLOWSHIP®

To Mom.

Without you, Pop does not become the model provider. Without your blessing, this book does not exist. You are a hero and I get the honor of calling you Mom.

Thank you.

FOREWORD

I have had the great fortune in my career to provide operational and financial leadership as a CFO to fast-growth startups and companies with billions in revenue and with global operations. With a masters degree in counseling and coaching certification from Duke Medicine I've also provided clinical services in private practice and at the Carolina Clinic Executive Health Center at UNC to a diverse set of clients. However, outside of being a husband and father the most rewarding work I have done is in leading a men's mentoring program. It was through one of these mentoring groups that I met Justin and learned his story, before this one that you are about to read even existed.

From the beginning of mentoring Justin, I observed his intentionality. It was a subject we talked about during the men's group to encourage mentees like Justin to love others well and with purpose. In true Justin fashion, with his "Lets Do This!" attitude, he latched on to this topic quickly.

Justin exudes this quality of intentionality as a husband to Amy, father to Penny and Edie, business leader, as a nationally certified coach, and leader in his church and community which now includes his own men's mentoring groups that you learn more about. He is honoring and paying forward to others the

Christian legacy his father, "Pop," sought to instill in him. It's not easy, and Pop was not perfect. This is why we as men often hide and shirk from our calling. But Pop was real, present, and left it all on the table for Justin, his family, and community. We now get to benefit from those life lessons captured in this read.

Justin didn't always have a clear calling with all the info-graphics and lessons you will see in this book. I witnessed a young man who was deliberate in his commitments and relation-ships. Over eighteen months I mentored him and celebrated his children's births and promotions in his career, and supported him through the hard life challenges that are vulnerably described in the following chapters.

Become a Provider is a guide for those who want to lay down a legacy of being there, being known, being loved, and loving others well. It is my great honor to collaborate with Justin in his desire that we all leave a legacy of intentionality that leaves no word unsaid or action regretted. Blessings on your provider journey!

-Tim Oakley

INTRODUCTION

Bob Goff told me to write this book. Well, indirectly.

I had just finished his inspirational *Love Does* bestseller with my men's group and we did what he asked his readers to do—call him! At the end of his book he provides his personal cell phone number and encourages readers to call him. Sure enough, when our group called, he answered. Skilled at handling calls from complete strangers, Bob went right into his element, quickly making conversation in his energetic and trademark whimsical style. After we told Bob that we enjoyed his book (something he probably heard a dozen times from other callers that same day) he turned the tables on us.

"You should write a book."

While Bob was on speakerphone to my entire men's group, I felt he was speaking directly to me. He encouraged us to write our story down because we all have a story and it's something our kids would run into a burning building to save from being lost.

Here is my story of taking the idea of *Love Does* through the lens of loving others by becoming a provider.

I believe in order to enjoy life to its fullest, and to make God smile the widest grin, we need to open our hands. In short, to be a provider by blessing and protecting others.

Everyone has something in hand to give. No matter income, gender, or marital status—*you* have something to give to others. The three goals of this book are to give you confidence that:

1. You have something in your hand to give (it's not empty!)
2. You can develop and build specific muscles to open up your gift for others (give it away)
3. You will discover a new joy in life providing for others (get it all back and more!)

Becoming a provider may mean nothing to you, or it may conjure up images of a working parent, bringing the income for the family. I invite you to start clean and explore this idea of becoming a provider afresh. The process of becoming a provider has changed my life and I want you to experience the same joy.

This book presents a biblical view of becoming a provider; how to define it and how to practically step into this role.

My journey of becoming a provider involved pain, death, and addressing my insecurities. My hope is to help you avoid some of this anguish by sharing my deeply personal story. I will share the most impactful lessons and advice I gathered along the way so you can turn my journey of the last few years into a quick read. However, the journey of becoming a provider is fine-tuned over a lifetime, so let's not wait to get started. I want you to enjoy life the way God intended now. Let's start developing and building muscles to help us open up our hands to others.

CHP

I USED TO THINK I HAD PLENTY OF TIME WITH MY LOVED ONES.
NOW I KNOW TODAY IS ALL I HAVE.

I stood at my desk and opened my laptop. The office was silent and empty as I prepared for the day. I was the first to arrive and the morning light was just beginning to fill the room.

I was entering my fourth year as CEO of a small tech company. We were making strides towards our ten-year vision by hiring a talented team, moving into a hip downtown co-working space and launching an exciting new product to the market. I was doing what they say to do, "planning my work and working my plan." I had even completed a pre-dawn workout to start the week off right. I settled into my standing desk, feeling energized about the week ahead.

I started writing out my to-do list for the day. A daily ritual to help me identify and prioritize my top three goals for the day.

Just then my phone broke the silence and vibrated.

I sighed, the distractions were already starting. My early morning routine was being threatened and I felt annoyed at this inconvenience. I glanced down at my phone preparing to swipe away the notification and then stopped.

It was a text message from my father, affectionately known as

Pop. The message simply read "CHP." This was code for "call house phone," and meant "I need to talk to you, but you have to call me." Pop didn't have outbound calling from his house phone, his resolute decision to save a couple bucks, despite the constant inconvenience. He still used an old school flip phone so his texts were short and sweet.

I was ready to jump into work and having a conversation with Pop this early in the morning was not on my to-do list. But then again, Pop had never texted so early in the morning.

I took a deep breath to move past the interruption in my day and called Pop, still thinking about all my responsibilities for the week ahead.

A man answered the landline, but it was not Pop's voice.

"This is Raymond. I'm here with your mom." He paused before delivering the shocking news. "Your dad died this morning."

My stomach dropped. My mind, numb to the news it had just heard, was unable to formulate any response. Finally, I uttered a weak acknowledgement through the phone. "What?" was all I could say.

Raymond, a close family friend, spoke matter of factly. "We've called the cops and your mom wanted me to call you. Would you like to speak to her?"

"Yes," I replied as my mind spun in circles. One-word responses were all I had to offer in this tragic moment.

This was supposed to be a normal Monday. A day which would fade away from memory from its standard weekly routines. However March 20, 2017 would turn into a day I can recall most vividly.

"Hi, honey," Mom struggled through tears. She began to fill me in on the details. Pop had had a heart attack early in the morning. It was quick and he was gone. I would learn more of the miraculous story later. He was only 67.

Mom continued, "Do you want to see Pop's body before the ambulance arrives?"

She was asking me if I would come take care of her.

I shielded my face from view in case anyone walked down the hallway. I gazed out the office window overlooking Main St. trying to process it all and what I should do. Downtown was bustling along, everyone in an angry rush to get to work, single-focused on the plans of the day. I had been just like them mere minutes ago.

None of that mattered anymore.

"No, Mom, don't wait on me to call the ambulance," I responded. "I'll be right there. I'm only 3 hours away. I love you."

I got off the phone and stood in the center of the empty office. I was thankful to be alone in this moment as I regrouped myself. Like Raymond, I went into a businesslike mindset. Everything had changed. I needed to prepare to leave the office immediately and sent out a message to my coworkers that my father had passed away and that I would be on bereavement leave. I sent a separate message to the Executive Team stating I was going on indefinite leave. With that, I packed my bags and exited the office much heavier than I had entered. I made my way to the parking deck and collapsed in my front seat.

I took a moment to send a group text message to my closest friends. I notified them that Pop had passed and that I was about to begin my journey back home. Similar to how Mom asked for help in her own way, I was asking these men to take care of me. I didn't need to ask for anything in particular, I was confident they would support me in prayer and however I would need. After sending this message I started up the car. I exited the empty parking deck towards the highway and started the drive to see Mom.

I then made the hardest calls I've ever had to make. First I called my brother and then my wife.

Thankfully my brother answered. He probably thought the same thing I did when I received a "CHP" text so early in the day. Something unusual must have prompted my call so out of the ordinary. After quickly asking my brother how he was doing, I told him I had some hard news to share.

This was the first time I'd said it out loud—"Pop passed away." Instead of delivering the news with Raymond's calm delivery, my voice cracked from emotion as I spoke to my brother.

It was in this moment that I realized I was going south on the highway when I needed to be going north.

John was as stunned as I had been just fifteen minutes earlier. As I turned the car around, my brother asked if he could pray. This spoke volumes to the man and character of my little brother. While I was fumbling to go the correct direction, his internal compass was pointed where it needed to be in this moment.

He prayed for our family and honored the legacy of Pop. I remember thinking how it was likely the first prayers for our family during this time of loss. My brother finished his prayer and I told him I was headed to see Mom and that I had not yet told my wife or our sister the news yet. He informed me that he too would be on his way after he packed up his wife and seven-month-old son.

I then tried calling my wife, Amy. No answer and I elected not to leave a message. I focused on driving the right way as I controlled my emotions.

The drive to see Mom was a blur. Sometimes I would find myself humming along to a song and then remember the news I had received. My mind was trying to protect me from the reality of the situation while my body was going through the motions.

One moment I would feel thankful and the other moment a darkness trying to overtake me. I would fight off this heaviness with memories of being with my brother and Pop just two weeks earlier for a guys weekend. Then I would think about my work and how everything was going to get done. There seemed to be a game of ping-pong going back and forth in my memories between positive and negative thoughts. Throughout the drive random memories of Pop would jump to the surface. My racing mind was interrupted when my phone rang. It was my wife, Amy, calling back.

"Hey," I said. "How are you and the girls?"

"We're fine." She sounded busy. Naturally she had no idea what had transpired. "We just finished their swim lessons and I'm packing them up in the car now."

I could hear my daughters in the background, laughing. Then it hit me.

How do I tell my daughters that their beloved Pop is gone?

Visualizing having this conversation with my oldest daughter was heartbreaking. How do you describe the concept of death to a three-year-old? How do you tell her someone that she knew and loved and that she just saw a couple weeks ago is now gone? How do you handle the sudden loss of the beloved grandfather who hand-made her a rocking horse and bought her first cowgirl hat? Then I was devastated with the thought that our one-year-old daughter would never know Pop.

How do you handle the sudden loss of your father, your example? Who do you become without the model patriarch?

"Amy, I need you to be strong for the girls." I was now in tears. I willed the words out the best I could and shared the news. Pop was gone. I informed her that I was on my way up to see Mom and asked if she could pack up the girls and head up whenever she could. She said she would pack up immediately and I knew she would. Only my wife could handle the tragic news, manage two girls under the age of four, and pack them up for an undetermined length of time—including funeral clothes—on such short notice.

After speaking with my wife I remember continuing the three-hour drive without making any stops. A couple calls and texts came in, some offering prayers and condolences, and some trying to work out business needs in my absence.

I went through the motions of that drive until I was stirred out of my slumber when a flash appeared on my dashboard. It was the gas light indicating I was low on fuel. I was only thirty minutes away, there was no way I was stopping. I pressed on, hoping to make it there before running out of fuel-both for the car and emotionally I was already drained. Just as I was regaining composure I turned onto Pop's gravel road. The possibility of potentially seeing his dead body brought a restless unease over me as I parked the car. I had finally arrived and my life, let alone my carefully prepared week, would never be the same.

THE GIFT OF BECOMING A PROVIDER

I USED TO THINK MY HAND WAS EMPTY. NOW I KNOW GOD IS
TOO GENEROUS TO LEAVE ME EMPTY HANDED.

An amazing transformation occurred in my life from the time I received that final "CHP" text and today. I've experienced a new sense of calling and purpose in my life. On the surface this makes no sense. The father I loved and respected is gone forever and I have the audacity to claim I am enjoying life more? Sounds downright heartless. However, my heart had to break to discover this truth and my hope through this book is that yours does not need to go through the fire to discover the same great opportunity in your life.

So, what's the secret? Become a provider.

Adopting a provider mindset has changed my life and I believe it can do the same for you. Whether you are single or married, male or female, I believe all can step into the fullness of who God designed you to be by becoming a *biblical provider*. A biblical provider is one who receives their provision from God and then provides for others. The passing of my father and the subsequent decisions, traumatic experiences, and career-changing decisions showed me the power of becoming a provider. Adopt this before you are faced with a crisis like the sudden passing of a parent, and you will be well prepared to handle the unexpected challenges life will throw at you.

A provider is defined as "one that provides." OK, so what does *provide* mean? Some definitions from Webster's are telling: *to make preparation to meet a need; to prepare in advance; to supply something for sustenance or support*[1]. The very title of being a provider is assuming action. It means both having foresight and doing the work. A provider is not a fly-on-the-wall, stagnant role in life. Before you start providing, you have to have something to give. Here is the great news. Each and every one of us has something to give. Imagine your hand not empty-handed but rather with something God has uniquely given you to provide for others. We all have something in our hands because God is a generous God.

Fortunately God does not have "good" and "bad" days when it comes to generosity. Unlike you and I who can be extremely generous one moment and then selfish the next, God is consistently generous. Scripture captures the generosity of God's character through creation and forgiveness when it says in Psalms 36:5-8,

> Your lovingkindness and graciousness, O LORD, extend to the skies, Your faithfulness [reaches] to the clouds. Your righteousness is like the mountains of God, Your judgments are like the great deep. O LORD, You preserve man and beast. How precious is Your lovingkindness, O God! The children of men take refuge in the shadow of Your wings. They drink their fill of the abundance of Your house; And You allow them to drink from the river of Your delights.[2]

Therefore, if we truly believe we serve a generous and loving God, we must believe that God provides for you and me. If you don't believe you have anything to give to others, nothing to provide, than you are spitting in God's face. You are claiming that the God who sent his son Jesus to this earth to sacrifice for you and me is not generous. Sound harsh? I want to make sure you know that it is not humble to think you don't have anything to give--it is sinful, as you are claiming God does not provide for you. Believing you don't have anything to provide is not believing in the very nature of God.

The great news is that if we accept the truth that God generously provides for us, we then have something to provide others. In order to earn the title of provider, we simply need to provide.

Here's what I hope for this short book: that you will commit to being a great provider based on the incredible, imperfect legacy of CL Thomas—"Pop," as he was known to his family. That you will know what providing means. That you will make a covenant to bless and protect anyone who needs your specific gifts—from a stranger on the side of the road to the kids in your home.

I want you to remember that providing on Earth is an imitation of Jesus—whose feet my father is sitting at right now.

I hope that, like Pop, you will see becoming a provider as a great adventure. Whether you have a strong or weak provider muscle, this book is for you to help improve and maximize how you provide. Let's start your journey of becoming a stronger provider. The people around you need you to develop into the provider God wants you to be and who you were designed to be.

A PROVEN PROCESS OF BECOMING A PROVIDER

I USED TO CARE ABOUT LEADERSHIP. NOW I AM FOCUSED ON
BECOMING A PROVIDER.

One of my life callings is to spread the good news that *anyone* can become a better provider and that this allows you to enjoy life more fully than ever before. As long as my relationship with God and my wife are healthy, I will be spreading this message and carrying on this work.

I have experienced first hand the transformation and joy of maturing from selfish living to provider living. What is even more exciting is that I have replicated this successful change outside of myself, by seeing this transformation through my small mentoring groups and individual coaching clients. Here are some quotes from men who have completed the provider journey with me:

- "The accountability aspect and the discipleship through the various books forced me to really look at my heart and ask how I could improve myself as a husband before seeking to improve my wife."
- "I feel more focused and discerning knowing what my role is supposed to be as a provider through the lens of God."
- "The activities required discipline because of the time

commitment. The discipline spilled over into other areas of my life like leading my wife, at work, and time with friends."

My prayer and hope is that by sharing my personal transformation and the wisdom shared to me through mentors, pastors, and parents that I can help you speed along your own journey of becoming the best provider you can be so you can discover the same joy.

We have already reviewed the dictionary definition of being a provider. Here is my provider equation:

$$\text{Provider} = \text{Bless} + \text{Protect.}$$

A provider is one who not only provides, but specifically provides blessings and offers protection to others. This is the proven provider process. If you can develop the habits and skills to consistently bless and protect others, you will grow into an effective and life-changing person to others.

I will share specific ways to develop "blessing" and "protecting" habits. First, I want to share how I discovered the provider equation.

POP'S FINAL LETTER

I USED TO PRACTICE MY OPENING PITCH. NOW I KNOW THE
TREASURE IS FOUND IN OUR FINAL WORDS.

I stirred out of bed, feeling restless. I quietly exited the dark guest bedroom so as not to awaken my wife or two girls who were all soundly sleeping. We were all staying with Mom as we sorted out what all needed to be done in the wake of Pop's death. In the pre-dawn hours of the morning, I tiptoed down the hall towards the kitchen trying to ensure Mom would also not be disturbed. As I settled down at the kitchen table I exhaled, trying to breathe some life into my weary body. After throwing myself into the logistics of the week, my hard outer shell was starting to crack from the beating waves of activity. From accountants, lawyers, financial advisors, and insurance agents, the meetings had been all consuming.

In between these meetings Mom, my siblings, and I had managed to meet together to discuss how we would honor Pop. We all agreed to host a public reception similar to an Irish wake to pay tribute to Pop and his life. I told my family I wanted to deliver a toast in Pop's honor. I had no idea what I wanted to say at the time when I volunteered, however I had a clear vision of standing in front of a crowd, welcoming them and sharing some remarks. We had all been very busy since this coffee shop discussion and I personally hadn't thought about what I would share in my toast.

Finally alone in the predawn darkness of Mom's kitchen, it was time to think and reflect on this important task at hand. Perhaps my most important public remarks I would make outside of my wedding vows. Now, without the distraction of a meeting or activity, the reality of Pop's passing was starting to penetrate my soul and become a reality. In two days I would speak on behalf of my family and deliver Pop's eulogy. How could I use this opportunity wisely? I hoped I would find some inspiration for this task at hand in order to appropriately honor Pop.

It was time to open the letter.

Two years earlier, I had received an envelope in the mail with Pop's instantly recognizable handwriting on it. I opened it up only to discover another, smaller envelope. It was sealed with simple instructions: "Put in a safety deposit box, open upon my death." This was classic Pop; no forewarning and no elaborate instructions. I called him up and asked if there was anything I should know about this mysterious letter. Pop simply responded to do what it said, and that was that. You didn't argue with Pop. I put it in my safety deposit box where it had remained.

My wife had retrieved the letter after I called with the news of Pop's death. This was an impressive feat considering she had to organize someone else to watch our kids while she ran out to the bank and carefully packed it up along with everything we needed for the week ahead. With all the activities and immediate demands of the moment, I had put this letter on the back burner. Now was the moment to finally open it and unveil its contents.

I searched for the letter and there it was, tucked away where Amy had packed it. The sun would not come up for a few more hours. I was thankful to have this quiet moment alone. I needed Pop's guidance and direction. As I slid my finger under the envelope flap, I was still robotically going through the steps. When my world suddenly changed without Pop I became callous to the events at hand to cope and address with whatever needed my attention. The letter however would not just be another to-do item to mark as completed. It would serve as a source of inspiration for my toast—and life moving forward.

Inside the envelope was a single sheet of paper, a handwritten letter from Pop. It had been intentionally prepared for this moment, addressed specifically to me, the oldest of three children. With a burst of adrenaline, I unfurled the crisp paper and read its contents:

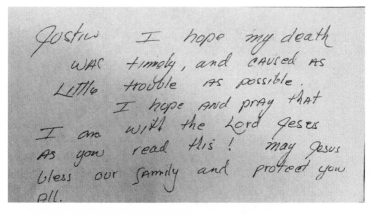

Pop's Final Letter. "Justin, I hope my death was timely and caused as little trouble as possible. I hope and pray that I am with the Lord Jesus as you read this! May Jesus bless our family and protect you all."

He signed it, "Love, Pop."

And that was not all. There was a drawing under his signature of where I could find cash at the house to pay for funeral expenses. Classic Pop! He had left with with words of inspiration and a treasure map! I was holding a precious gift in my hands. Beyond the financial gift, I had been given a more precious asset, a short benediction to carry on in life. It was direct and to the point—which was how Pop always communicated.

What would you write to your child at the end of your life? How would you speaking blessing over them?

We can look at the apostle Paul for how his final words

revealed what he thought was his most important message. Here he is In Acts 20:25, 32-37 leaving friends for what Paul believes will be the final time:

> Now I know that none of you among whom I have gone about preaching the kingdom will ever see me again...**Now I commit you to God and to the word of his grace**, which can build you up and give you an inheritance among all those who are sanctified. I have not coveted anyone's silver or gold or clothing. You yourselves know that these hands of mine have supplied my own needs and the needs of my companions. In everything I did, I showed you that by this kind of hard work we must help the weak, remembering the words the Lord Jesus himself said: **'It is more blessed to give than to receive.'** When Paul had finished speaking, he knelt down with all of them and prayed. They all wept as they embraced him and kissed him.[1] (emphasis mine)

In reference to this passage, Pastor Tim Keller reflects how Paul's words demonstrates what he held closest to his heart. Paul believed there was nothing more important to share with his friends than this: that to the degree to which we understand the gospel of grace we will live a radical life of generosity.[2]

Both Paul and Pop preached generosity through their final words. Pop's final letter demonstrated his selflessness. He didn't want his death to be a burden. Even in the first few days, those raw and sensitive days, I was experiencing the soothing feeling of knowing Pop had thoughtfully planned and prepared his family for life without him. He had a will and left a debt-free estate. This was all before I had received the treasure map drawing! This thoughtful planning was even more incredible, considering Pop worked in the low-margin retail furniture business his entire career.

Pop had indeed accomplished his wish to cause "as little trouble as possible." He was showing me how to think of others even through his death. I would have probably written a how-to

list for my firstborn, something to make me feel smart and impor-
tant--and that's even assuming I would have had the wisdom and
foresight to write a letter! Here was Pop surprising me with

1. having a letter prepared for me, and
2. having the focus on our family and not himself.

As I reread the short letter again and studied the drawing, I
smiled at the thought of Pop with Jesus. It became real to me right
then that he was in Heaven. *In Heaven!* This place I supposedly
believed in as a Christian but never really pictured anyone actually enjoying. I rested in that vision for a moment and made some
tea as the orange sun started to peer over the mountains of Blacks-
burg, Virginia. I had received the inspiration for my toast thanks
to Pop's letter.

While the beginning and middle of Pop's letter touched me,
the closing line became my new rally cry in life. *"May Jesus bless
our family and protect us all."* I couldn't just follow the steps in my
own strength, I needed Jesus to bless and protect me through this
first week of Pop's passing and my upcoming toast.

I started writing my toast about Pop with a new energetic
focus. As the sun turned from orange to a yellow hue, I folded
back the letter to keep safe. I knew exactly what I would say for
my final remarks about Pop. I could only hope and pray they
would have a similar weight and impact as Paul and Pop showed
me through their final words on the importance of generosity and
giving to others. I wanted my toast to be a gift to those in
attendance.

While the letter was Pop's final writing I had, I also could
learn more lessons from his final spoken words before his death. I
was beginning to discover and appreciate not slick opening lines,
but the thoughtfulness and power of final words.

5

POP'S FINAL WORDS

I USED TO THINK MOMENTS WERE EITHER MEANINGLESS OR
LIFE-CHANGING. NOW I KNOW THEY ARE ALL DIVINE.

L et me pause and share a little more about Pop and his last days, going back to the day of his death and my arrival at his house.

I had just completed the drive from my work in North Carolina to our family mountain lodge in Floyd, Virginia. My heart was racing, as I gripped the cold, brass front door handle and stepped into the open living room. I had no idea what to expect. Would Pop's lifeless body still be there?

My first image was a man sitting upright on the sofa. My eyes adjusted to the soft, indoor lighting and I noticed the stoic figure was Raymond, our friend who had delivered the news to me just three hours earlier. Then I saw Mom and we embraced in the living room.

"They took his body," Mom sobbed in my arms. I was relieved; I had no desire to see Pop's lifeless body. All I could do was hang on to Mom. My mind was racing through all memories. I specifically thought about how I was standing in this same spot just two weeks earlier with Pop and my brother for our guys weekend. We ended our time together holding hands in prayer. Now I was holding on to my weeping mother. Pop had prayed a blessing over my brother and me and ended with his prayer asking Jesus to "be with us all the days of our lives."

After a few moments Mom released her grip and Raymond came over and shook my hand. I thanked him for being there. Sometimes the best gift is simply being present, and I was certainly thankful for his calming presence. We all sat down on the sectional, stunned at the moment.

Once seated, Mom started to share what had happened. I was impressed that she wanted to share, let alone speak at all. She was visibly shaken, heartbroken but there was a tangible feeling of strength coming from her body language. She had a peaceful tone as she started to recall how her husband, my father--"Pop"--had died in this very room just hours ago. Unbeknownst to me I was sitting in his final resting place, the exact spot where he breathed his last breath.

Mom must have intuitively sensed that I desperately wanted to know what happened to Pop. How could he be gone? What had happened? She saved me the effort of asking for details. The story of Pop's final and divine moments. Regardless of what you personally believe, his last moments were just incredible.

She sat with me, teary-eyed, and started to share the events that just changed our reality forever. I was in a state of shock, but tried breathing slowly to help me focus on her words. "We went out to dinner last night, and it was a fun night out together." I smiled to myself. I knew exactly what Mom meant. When Pop was in a bad mood, everyone could feel it. He did not hide anything; he was direct and authentic. On the one hand what you saw was what you got with Pop and on the other hand, he lived a much richer and more complex life than what many would believe. This was new insight I had only recently learned --more to come on that later. However, I did not let myself linger in the past and once again concentrated on Mom's words as she unpacked the story of Pop's final day.

"We were driving in silence back from a really pleasant dinner together in Pop's car and then..." Mom paused before starting again. "And then...out of nowhere, he said to me, 'Ya know, I'm not going to live forever.'"

"This was so out of the blue and I made a joke of it, saying, 'Of course you are! You are going to take care of me,'" Mom replied with a laugh.

After a few more moments of silence, they shifted the conversation and reviewed their plans for the following day. They were going to drive into the city for a fun outing of eating and shopping together. Before leaving for the city in the morning they needed to pick up Mom's car from the mechanics.

Mom thought they were all set with their plans and then Pop surprised her again. "Let's get the car now," he said.

"Tonight?" Mom asked. It was late. She was full and tired from a delicious meal and evening out together. Plus the shop would be closed.

"Why wait?" he said. Instead of getting Mom's car the next day, why not get it right now? So Pop went twenty minutes out of his way to the mechanic and pulled into the dark shop. He knew the car was ready and how the honor system worked. He stepped out and wrote what would be his final check, thus ensuring he did not owe anyone anything. A man of integrity, honoring all his commitments and obligations until the very end. The keys were waiting for him in the unlocked car and they drove home separately in the two cars back to his house.

Mom continued the story. "After watching a show, we went to bed, expecting to start the next day as normal. And then..." There was that pause again. Mom needed a moment before continuing on. "And then around 4:30 a.m., Pop got out of bed." I felt a tension of wanting to stop Mom from reliving the tragic moment that was mere hours removed and also desperately wanting her to find the strength to continue. Fortunately Mom's strength won and she continued sharing. "When he got up he said, 'It hurts right here.'" Mom re-enacted Pop pointing to his chest.

Mom went on to describe how they moved out of the bedroom and into the living room to rest on the sectional. Pop was calm but kept saying it hurt in the middle of his chest and that his arms were tingling. Mom asked if they should go to the hospital. Pop shook his head and asked Mom to find the medical diagnosis book in the house.

It was a serious moment and they both knew it. No diagnostic book was needed.

"I told him, 'Your chest hurts and your arms are tingling—we don't need a book to tell us you're having a heart attack.'" Mom shared how she was mentally preparing to leave for the hospital. She started to gather her items for the trip into the community hospital. Meanwhile Pop was praying out loud in a calm fashion that helped to soothe Mom's anxiousness. He was reciting scriptures that were near to his heart and written on the inside of his well worn leather Bible.

After a couple minutes of praying Pop paused. "It feels better." He rested on the edge of the sectional and then asked Mom to put wood in the stove to heat the living room.

It was cool, the sun still had not risen. Mom got up off the sofa, walked over to wood pile by the fireplace and placed a new log in the stove. As she was leaning by the stove she heard Pop's final spoken words, "You did a good job."

Mom looked up from the stove to see Pop smiling and sitting upright on the sofa with his hands extended to the sky. A moment later his hands fell and crossed over his eyes. Pop was gone.

"His last words to me," Mom continued as she spoke directly to me, "his last words were so special. I took 'good job' to mean *well done* as a wife, mother, and friend. I just laid there next to his body crying and praying." Mom then smiled and recalled, "Pop would joke with me early in our marriage about needing a wife to keep the fire going while he was at work. As a city girl growing up in San Francisco, this was not something that came naturally to me."

We both knew in that moment Pop had picked the perfect wife to put the final log on the fire. Once again I was reminded of the power of final words. Whether reading his final letter to me or heating Pop's final words of encouragement to Mom, there was a consistent theme of providing for others. I reflected how even in death Pop was giving to us. It was a challenging observation to accept. If he could do this in death, what more are we who are still healthy and living called to do? I felt convicted. Pop did so much for us; had I appreciated his example? These questions would continue to convict me throughout the grieving process. I was starting to appreciate how each moment is divine.

6

MY FINAL REMARKS

I USED TO THINK IT WAS FUN BEING ON STAGE. NOW I KNOW
THE STAGE DEMANDS PREPARATION.

I t was time to deliver my final toast to Pop. The date was Friday, March 24, 2017, four days since his passing. After hearing Mom recount Pop's final moments and opening his final letter to me, I was more impressed with the man I called Pop. He had solidified his legacy through these final actions and I wanted to honor his life and example.

I had volunteered for this opportunity and I didn't want to squander the moment. Of all the activities that I had co-labored in since Pop's death, this was the pinnacle moment.

What would someone say about you at your funeral? Better yet, what would you *want* them to say? This question went from a theoretical one to something I truly started to consider in preparation of Pop's toast.

I wanted to honor Pop's life with authentic and meaningful words, not empty metaphors or forced expressions to try to soothe over the pain of loss. I wasn't trying to elicit cheap, shallow laughs. I wanted to honor the man through my prepared remarks. Pop had demonstrated a level of preparedness, even before a sudden death, and I wanted to honor that characteristic trait in my toast.

My family had done an excellent job organizing the logistics, given the circumstances, to host a private family breakfast and then an afternoon public reception to pay their respects to Pop. We reserved the upstairs bar area at a local restaurant for the reception. Since we'd decided on a bar setting, I elected not to call my prepared remarks a eulogy. It was more like a toast. A toast to Pop's life.

Although it took me hours to write, my toast was one page in length. I challenged myself to pick one characteristic trait to highlight. My goal was to leave everyone with one simple message and image of Pop. He was the model provider. I would honor Pop the provider through my prepared remarks.

I was in an unfamiliar role of speaking at a funeral/wake for the first time. I had no idea what it would feel like and if I could get through it. To help strengthen my resolve, I carried Pop's Bible with me and wore his old leather vest that I found in his closet.

I arrived in the reception hall and greeted people as they arrived. A slideshow of classic Pop pictures played while we all mingled making small talk. Everyone admired Pop's drawings and woodworking pieces that we had put on display for people to appreciate his many artistic talents. It was nice to see so many people from different eras of Pop's life. Everyone was gracious and yet still struggling with the surprise that Pop was really gone. After an hour or so I told everyone to grab a drink from the bar for a toast in five minutes.

A few minutes later I stepped onto the stage. I was standing in an erected DJ booth area and was about to give the presentation of my life: a toast to my father's legacy. True, it was a nontraditional setting, yet was just right for who Pop was. It was the type of funeral he would have wanted to attend.

When I took to the stage the bar activity stopped and all eyes were on me. No more chit chat or nervous energy could be heard, just felt. For the first time, I felt the weight of being on stage.

As the moment became more real to me, I looked out on the hundred or so people before me, and caught my brother's eye. I looked down at my one-pager to gather my emotions. Now it was my turn to share final remarks.

I was confident in the words I was about to share. Yet I was unprepared for the emotions of the moment.

I looked back at the crowd and welcomed them on behalf of Mom, my sister, my brother, and our entire family. Then I started to share the following prepared remarks.

Thank you for joining us today for this memorial.

It is my honor to share some brief remarks about my father, Calvin Thomas.

I want to focus our time together on one specific trait and role that he excelled at in life.

That word and role is *provider*.

What did he provide?

On the surface he provided sixty-seven years of memories from his time here.

On the surface he provided for his wife for thirty-four years.

On the surface he provided financially for his family by running the furniture store for thirty-plus years.

But what Pop really loved was simply providing for his family and those in need.

I stopped to gather myself. My voice cracked as I was surprised my emotions were welling up. I shouldn't have been taken this off guard, but for some reason I was not expecting to be gasping for air. I needed to reach deeper than I had ever done before to gain composure and share what I had so desperately wanted to articulate to the waiting crowd. I breathed in and out to regain my strength and carried on.

Here are just a few of the things Pop did in the last year alone to provide:

He provided a home for my sister and her family, laboring in it with his own two hands, customizing it for the unique needs of his special-needs grandson. This project showed off his wide-ranging craftsman skills and more importantly his fatherly love for my sister.

Three weeks ago he invited my brother and me to meet at his house to hear his life story. During this time he encouraged us to ask any questions we wanted to. I will forever be grateful for that day and what we shared together.

Just last week he picked up a hitchhiker in Floyd, whom he remembered delivering furniture to during his furniture company days. After dropping him off at his house Pop gave the passenger his nice warm wool gloves from the car and some money. (During all this my mom was in the car! It's a good thing she was, as she served as translator/megaphone for the hard-of-hearing Pop, as she often did, to turn the passenger's thick country accent into coherent thoughts.)

And lastly and even more recently, the night before his death, Pop provided a final meal for my mom (out to eat of course) and, just to put the final exclamation mark on his legacy as provider, on their way back from dinner, instead of waiting until the next day, Pop picked up Mom's car from the mechanics on Sunday night, before breathing his last breath by her side Monday morning.

Pop never waited until the next day.

He always provided today.

Please join me in a toast.

To Pop; the provider who modeled his life after the ultimate Provider, Jesus Christ. Today we celebrate the fact that he is being provided for in Heaven.

To Pop!

I lifted my drink in the air as everyone shouted, "To Pop!" I had teared up during my remarks, but somehow managed to hold it together and deliver the message in full.

My high school speech and drama teacher, who was a close family friend, came up to me after the toast and told me it was "perfect in every way." I appreciated those words. I had spoken the truth, shared authentically, showed genuine emotion, and ended with a message of thankfulness. I did the best I could. I gave it all I had.

————

What would you say about your father or close family member if you were asked to share a toast on their behalf? Better yet, have you thought about what they'd say of you?

With adrenaline still flowing, I saw my sister and we embraced. My sister and I were not close at the time, however we immediately brushed all that baggage aside. As I held on to her, my eyes welled. After hugging my sister, I went to the bathroom for a moment alone.

I felt I had nothing left to give. I just sat in the stall and realized on the one hand it doesn't matter how low you might feel, people continue to need you. The goal is to figure out how to go from the low and refuel to consistently be a provider for those in your life. I wasn't sure how I could provide anymore than I had just done in my toast, let alone how I would have the strength to return to the room of people.

I thought of my mom, my sister, my brother, my wife who were all out there in the room. I needed to be there with them. I was sure they were going through their own low moment. I realized this is what being a provider was. This was blessing and protecting others.

————

I had used the phrase "give it all you got" in the past on sports teams, MBA classrooms, and business events. Now I knew what that phrase really meant, and what it authentically felt like. Previous moments of giving it all I had were mere glimpses of this toast moment. I used to think it was fun being on stage. Now I knew what the stage requires: preparation.

After delivering the toast, I wanted to become a provider like Pop. I wasn't just going through the motions of the required meetings that everyone needs to attend after a death. I wanted to be much more than that. The family needed it and I wanted to learn how to carry on this character strength that I had just shared in Pop's toast. I wanted to spend more time reflecting on Pop's life, scripture, and lessons from mentors to help me become a provider in my own way. I returned to the reception and was received warmly and with care. I realized *they* were providing for *me* in this moment. I would need all this support as I had another unexpected challenge ahead.

7

BREAKDOWN

I USED TO THINK I COULD FOOL ANYONE. NOW I KNOW I WAS
THE FOOL HIDING BEHIND A MASK.

.

S hortly after delivering the toast, I returned home to North Carolina with my family. I hadn't fully realized the harsh new reality of life without a father. The busyness of the previous couple of weeks had distracted me from facing this new reality. I put on a mask to just get things done that needed to be done. In fact, I was mistaken for the family lawyer at the bank based on my demeanor, questions, and the fact that I was carrying an old school briefcase!

I could not wear the mask forever. Fortunately I had amazing people in my life who helped to gently remove it.

First, Mom gave me a book on grieving.[1] This was an unexpected gift. I should have been the one providing for her! With a strong sense of mother's intuition, she knew I needed support through my own grieving process. It proved to be the first step in loosening my mask. I would have never bought this book on my own, yet I was comforted by its mere presence on my night stand. It provided a resource of encouraging words and an explanation on how the grieving process is like the changing seasons. There are natural cycles of grief and they will feel unique--some more comfortable than others--like the weather. Winter is not forever, and to honor whatever season you must simply go through it. You can't skip winter for summer. You must go through the appropriate season of life for the ecosystem to work. Likewise for our souls. The book allowed me to appreciate how difficult survival seasons can lead to growth and rebirth.

Second, my friend Brad encouraged me to journal. I told him the incredible story of Pop's final words to Mom and he simply, yet forcefully, told me to write it all down. I'm so grateful he prompted me to make time for this journaling exercise. Not only did it help me in writing this book with accuracy, it allowed me to reflect on the divine nature of Pop's passing and all the lessons I was being exposed to and learning.

After my two weeks of bereavement leave, I journaled in a private notebook as Brad suggested. I spent hours writing. I reflected on all the details and moments after receiving the "CHP" text message from Pop's phone. The volume of pages felt more like a full memoir, yet the content only spanned a period of twelve hours. I then made an outline of all the events the week of Pop's passing and was struck by how much I had done and how little I had rested.

Finally, my mask was fully removed during a coffee meeting with my pastor. Pastor Reggie isn't just a pastoral figure in my life, he is a friend. We met over a decade ago during a pick-up basketball game when he was a campus minister and I was a recent college graduate. He knew me and was not fooled by my claims that I was fine. We had spoken a couple times on the phone after Pop's passing, but this would be our first in-person meeting since I had returned home. It started out similar to our previous conversations, but then something snapped in me.

"How are you and the family doing?" Reggie asked me as we settled into our chairs at a popular cafe. We were sitting outside on a cool spring day.

"We are good. It's been amazing to see how God held us all together during this time." I started to recount the major recent events in a methodical fashion, and then something unexpected happened. I broke down.

Tears started to flow uncontrollably. Snot coming out, the whole nine yards. I had a single napkin to try to control it all, but it was no match for the sheer volume of tears. The dam had broken loose. I could feel the other customers look over at me. I felt like I was making a scene. It didn't matter, I couldn't wear the mask any longer. Pastor Reggie gave me the space and time I needed before continuing. Honestly I'm surprised he didn't run to get more napkins, just so he didn't have to witness my blubbering mess! Through it all, he was showing me how to be there for a friend in need. I could feel the support, he didn't need to say anything.

I eventually managed to squeak out a more honest response. "It's been tough, Reggie."

I gained my composure when I started to share how I was inspired by Pop's legacy of being a great example of being a provider. He listened intently and then suggested I explore Psalm 23. This surprised me. I associated this famous passage with funerals and death, not being a provider. In fact, I had been given a laminated copy of Psalm 23 from the funeral home as a gift.

Pastor Reggie encouraged me to read Psalm 23 again, but this time through the lens of being a provider. I took his words to heart. This meeting was just what I needed to process the death of Pop, acknowledge the pain, and pursue the mantle of being a provider. Now that my mask was removed I could start to pursue this question of how to become a provider.

8

PSALM 23

I USED TO THINK I UNDERSTOOD THE BIBLE AS A WHOLE. NOW I KNOW I WILL SPEND MY LIFE DISCOVERING HIDDEN GEMS IN ITS PAGES.

I went back home and read Psalm 23 again, now with a genuine curiosity about how this related to being a provider. The passage reads:

The Lord is my shepherd;
I shall not want.
He makes me to lie down in green pastures;
He leads me beside the still waters.
He restores my soul;
He leads me in the paths of righteousness
For His name's sake.

Yea, though I walk through the valley of the
    shadow of death,
I will fear no evil;
For You are with me;
Your rod and Your staff, they comfort me.

You prepare a table before me in the presence
    of my enemies;
You anoint my head with oil;

> My cup runs over.
>
> Surely goodness and mercy shall follow me
> All the days of my life;
> And I will dwell in the house of the Lord
> Forever.[1]

I was still grasping to connect this chapter with being a provider. To dive deeper into this well-known chapter, I opened up the Wycliffe Bible Commentary and my perspective began to expand when I read the following (emphasis mine):

> As a **song of trust**, this psalm has no peer. It is impossible to estimate its effect upon man through the centuries. Grief, sadness, and doubt have been driven away by this strong affirmation of faith. Peace, contentment, and trust have been the **blessings** upon those who have come to share the psalmist's sublime confidence. While the language is simple and the meaning clear, no one has been able to exhaust the message of the poem or improve upon its quiet beauty.[2]

For the first time, I realized how this scripture beautifully describes blessing and protecting. The "song of trust" implies *protection*. The *blessings* described in Psalms 23 are confidently promised. Jesus even called himself the "Good Shepherd" in John 10: "I am the good shepherd. I lay down my life for the sheep." I was now starting to appreciate how Psalm 23 positioned Jesus as our model provider, one who blesses his sheep by selflessly giving of himself to earn the trust of his sheep. Since we are called to imitate Jesus (1 Corinthians 11:1, 1 Peter 2:21) we too are called to become the shepherd, the provider.

I continued to explore Psalm 23 through the lens of being a provider, specifically how my father described it as blessing and protecting others.

Protecting

Psalm 23:1-4

God's protector qualities are laid out in Psalm 23 1-4. God is the shepherd. A faithful shepherd is the "epitome of tender care and continuing watchfulness. The sheep instinctively trust the shepherd to provide for them." What a beautiful description and visual of being a provider. You can't protect someone until they trust you. We need to demonstrate a commitment to watching over others like the shepherd watches over his sheep. Someone strong enough to protect, yet tender enough for the "flock" to trust his guidance. Or, as Wycliffe describes in his Psalms 23 commentary, "He leads into rest and reviving, into the struggles of life and through the dangerous places. The shepherd thus provides for the needs of life and protects from the fear of danger."

Blessing

Psalm 23:5-6

Then, the blessing is outlined in the remaining two verses of Psalm 23. The chapter highlights a gracious host extending hospitality to guests with food, oil, and a grand party. The verses promise the guests will be filled with God's blessings. It is important to know that "the greatest blessing is an intimate *fellowship* with God through continued worship of Him."[3]

———

I had Pop's letter highlighting the concept of Jesus blessing and protecting our family and now Psalm 23 describing these same characteristics with beautiful imagery. I had goosebumps. The equation *Provider = Bless + Protect* was etched in my mind as truth. It was no longer just inspiring words for my toast, it was described in the Bible! I felt I had stumbled upon a hidden, deep truth in life.

Pop's life had been all about providing for others, and his letter called me to bless and protect like Jesus. Thanks to the nudging of my pastor and the Holy Spirit, I'd turned to Psalm 23 laying out a biblical picture of what it means to bless and protect, to result in ultimate fellowship.

I started to read scripture and pray each morning after returning home from Pop's funeral. Mom gave me Pop's Bible to take with me and I decided it would be better used reading rather than preserved away on a shelf. As I opened Pop's Bible I noticed his daily prayer was written on the inside cover. Pop recited this prayer every morning. Mom would hear him say it in the shower, or in the kitchen when he was preparing breakfast. He would always start his day out with this prayer he had written based on verses that changed his life. Below is an image of the first part of the prayer that struck me:

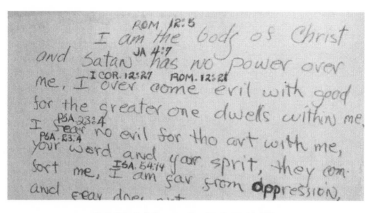

Part of Pop's daily prayer found tucked in his Bible

I was stunned—another divine moment. Here was Psalm 23 highlighted for me in Pop's prayer. I could see the specific verses that spoke to Pop including Psalm 23:4 as he prayed, "I fear no evil for thou art with me, your word and your spirit they comfort me." I loved the rawness of this prayer. All of its misspellings and imperfections made it more genuine to me. I was beginning to appreciate how much the psalms inspired Pop and why he included them in his daily prayer. It had helped shape him from a selfish man to the shepherd, the provider I knew and respected. Prayer was a key element of his personal development and ongoing commitment to becoming a provider.

A Covering

Take this psalm deep into your soul and trust the Shepherd to provide for you as you learn to provide for others. Pop depended on God's covering to provide moment by moment. This daily habit of praying a portion of Psalm 23 over his life taught me how I should make scripture and prayer a reality in my life, something that actually influenced my day and aided in my growth and desire to become a provider.

9

REFLECTING ON POP'S LIFE

I USED TO VALUE TAKING ACTION ABOVE ALL ELSE. NOW I HAVE
LEARNED THE IMPORTANCE OF REFLECTION.

"D o you think your dad thought of himself as a generous
person?"

I paused. My friend Matt went straight to his question. Silence fell over our phone conversation as I gathered my
thoughts. Matt didn't need my feedback. He confidently
answered his own question: "Because I know I could have asked
him for anything and he would have given it to me."

I smiled, thinking back to my toast and sharing the story of
Pop giving the hitchhiker his nice wool gloves and cash after
dropping him off home. Of course Pop was an extremely
generous person.

That conversation with Matt motivated me to dive deeper into
the habits and characteristics in Pop's life that made him a model
provider. What does a modern shepherd figure look like?
Generosity was certainly a defining element of being a provider.
What else constituted a model provider?

After my phone call with Matt I stepped into my daughters'
playroom and sat down in front of their whiteboard. I wanted to
tease out this thought and explore a provider's characteristics.
The whiteboard was set in a wooden easel that was handmade by

Pop for my daughters—another great example of his generosity. Reading the "Love Pop" inscription on the inside of the frame, I opened a blue marker to capture my thoughts.

I was searching for a roadmap; practical habits that I could create and personalize in order to carry on Pop's legacy as a provider. I had been blessed and protected by Pop. He helped to bring the shepherd figure to life. I wanted to do the same for others.

I wrote *Biblical Provider* at the top. I then made two columns. I labeled one column blue—*Bless*—and in orange, *Protect*. I started brainstorming the habits and characteristics that best represented these characteristics. It was a moment of inspiration. All the recent reflection time on Pop's life, Psalm 23, and my journaling produced story after story of what made Pop ... well, Pop. He lived life with an authentic confidence. He knew who he was and whom he served. Nothing others said or did could intimidate him or his beliefs.

During my MBA studies, my professors stressed the importance of identifying only a few but vital goals for a company's success. I tried to take this same strategic approach with brainstorming the most critical elements of becoming a provider. I challenged myself to consider only the top three to five habits that I could work on to bless others and the three to five habits to protect others.

In only a few minutes I was able to come up with a list of the top ways I saw Pop bless and protect others. I smiled as I looked at my scribbled notes on the kids' whiteboard. This is what I needed! A practical—but lofty—list of habits to try to implement in order to become the best provider I could be, rooted in the Christian faith.

How Pop Blessed Us

- His presence was a gift. He could be counted on in times of trouble and he pursued us.
- He vulnerably shared his remarkable story at the end of his life. (More on that in chapter 26)
- He gifted Mom with the words she needed in letters, frequent affirmation, and with his final breath.

How Pop Protected Us

- He was always known to keep a full gas tank, cash on hand, and emergency equipment in his car.
- He kept strong by working on his property.
- He was a man of his word, even when it almost cost him everything. He saw a liar and a thief as "one and the same"—a favorite catchphrase of his.

How Pop Combined the Two

- As Matt testified, he was perpetually generous and took wisdom on his finances from the Bible.
- He was a man of prayer first and foremost.

Now that I had summed up how Pop had blessed and protected our family, our community, and strangers in need, I needed to walk it out.

I had never intentionally desired to become a provider. I wanted to be a great husband, father, business leader, and friend. Before this moment, the idea of "becoming a provider" had never been a priority. However, I now felt a calling that would only increase its intensity.

I wanted to not only carry on the legacy of Pop, I wanted to step into the calling that I believed God had set before me. I had been provided for in so many ways throughout my life and especially through Pop's death. I was ready to become the provider.

I snapped a picture of the whiteboard before the kids got home and started to think of creating a visual guide that would last longer.

After all, I would need time to master these traits!

10

THE FELLOWSHIP IDEA

After spending time individually reflecting on Pop's life and discovering some of the characteristic traits that I wanted to develop, I was prompted to extend this research beyond myself. My plan was to test my whiteboard session and discover how best to add provider traits into my life through self-experimentation, learning from experts in a variety of disciplines, and scripture. As I was considering where to start first with this experiment of discovering how to become a provider like Pop, I was nudged by the Holy Spirit. It gets even more strange. The idea came in the shower. As if out of a movie, the word *fellowship* rushed into my consciousness in a sudden way that I could not ignore.

That's a weird word, right? Especially since I was thinking of trying to become a provider. What does "fellowship" have to do with that? I had never received a fellowship or even used that word in my vocabulary. It wasn't related to anything I was doing in work or life. However the weight of the word stayed with me. I had no doubt that this word came from God. Given all the divine encounters and stories surrounding Pop's life and death, I could not ignore this moment or this word. Perhaps God could speak into my life the way I had seen in Pop's life and death.

I said a quick prayer about what all this meant. "What does this word mean? Why have you given me this word, God?"

Over the next few days the word "fellowship" turned into taking my individual provider journey and extending it to a group, a special fellowship in honor of Pop. Rather than exploring how to climb the provider mountain like a John Wayne figure going at it alone, I sensed a different path was being laid out before me to become a provider. It would be the same mountain to climb but I would be journeying with others. I started to get more consumed and committed to this fellowship idea. I would name the group after Pop—the CL Thomas Fellowship.

I had the benefit of personally benefiting from a variety of people and groups in my life. I had worked with executive coaches, sales coaches, health coaches, Christian mentors, and pastors. Even the high standards of my men's group inspired me. I wanted to take everything I had benefited from and provide it to the fellowship.

I shared the idea with my wife. She smiled and assumed it was something I would eventually do. However, I really got her attention when I told her my full vision. I wanted to take a sabbatical from my career and concentrate on launching the CL Thomas Fellowship full time, at least for a season of life. I was serious about making this group as special and meaningful as possible. She was on board—as long as the work sabbatical ended before we ran out of money. I accepted those terms and pressed on with planning the fellowship!

This fellowship prompted me to think more high-level about my career. In the wake of the sudden loss of my father, I had to face it: what did I want to accomplish in my life? What would be my legacy? Would I just go home and carry on with business as usual? I picked up a copy of the toast I gave about Pop. I had been able to see so clearly what Pop stood for and the legacy he left for me. I believed the fellowship was the answer and I just needed to put some more thought and planning around the launch. I was confident I would figure out the career question. I believed the fellowship deserved my full attention.

————

The act of returning to the office became therapeutic for me. It was a critical part in my provider journey. I needed to walk back to the location where I received the news of Pop's passing and face my old reality with my new reality. Wherever the "hard place" is for you in your own life, sometimes you just have to step into it to move on.

After my MBA program I was given an incredible opportunity to become CEO of a small tech company of ten people in Durham, NC. It was a fifteen-year-old established business needing some new energy--just what I wanted. It was a real-world opportunity to implement the strategic lessons from the classroom and put them into practice. For nearly five years I partnered with the founder, CTO, and entire team to help stabilize the business and rebuild. It was the most challenging and rewarding work I had done to date. It stretched me beyond what I knew was possible and humbled me along the way.

I experienced all the highs and lows of running a small business. From cash crunches, hires, fires, and the thrill of winning new clients, it was a wild ride. I felt that my time was coming to an end. I had served as a "bridge CEO" to give the founder a break and now that he was rejuvenated he was the best person to lead the company again. I prayed for wisdom on my next steps. For now, it was time to go back to my CEO duties.

I reflected how the last couple of weeks had been a gift. I had been able to celebrate and honor Pop's legacy as a provider. I had received a creative spark of inspiration to start the CL Thomas Fellowship and felt the love and support of family and friends in deep and meaningful ways.

You learn a lot through tragedy. It exposes your foundation, your beliefs, strengths, and weaknesses.

What a change in just a couple of weeks. I was now seriously considering resigning as CEO and leaving my old career—and old life—behind.

11

SHARING THE VISION

I USED TO THINK IT WAS IMPORTANT TO JUST HAVE A VISION.
NOW I KNOW YOU ALSO NEED A PLAN TO GO WITH YOUR
VISION.

I wanted to tell the leadership team my transition plans as soon as I returned from bereavement leave. Fortunately for me, I'm married to a wise woman. I asked my wife for her advice before I told anyone else or made any huge decisions. Amy encouraged me to first take some time to process this idea further and better prepare for action. I'm glad she did. During that time the word *honor* kept arising in my thoughts.

I took honor to mean leaving the tech company honorably— not bailing on them when they most needed me or leaving work undone. I started praying for a healthier sales pipeline for the business while I was out on bereavement leave.

———

I was standing at my desk for the first time since Pop passed. It was now two weeks to the day since I learned the news and once again this was not just another Monday. My body was present, but I felt like a shell of my former self. Waiting for the team to come in brought a mix of anxiety and eagerness to get back to normalcy—whatever that looked like.

I was positioned in the same spot where I had received my

final "CHP" text message from Pop's number. I cleared my throat as I tried to act normal. The team would be in soon. I was carrying a heaviness with me as I opened my laptop. Two weeks ago I was full of energy, planning my day and week. Today I was just trying to make it through. I was not ready to get back to work.

Instead of forcing my mind to think about the current sales, hiring, and product launch plans, I drifted my eyes towards the window, took a moment to try to reflect on my time away from the office. I had been tested and remained standing. True, I felt exhausted, yet in general I was proud of how I had acted in the wake of Pop's death.

Now here I was; I had returned to the hard place, the exact spot I'd gotten the worst news of my life. I was facing my new reality in the wake of my old one. I couldn't help but be a different person, even as I stood in the same spot with the same responsibilities I had just a mere two weeks prior.

I reflected on my tentative plan to step down as CEO and leave indefinitely to launch the fellowship. Although the timing felt right, I didn't want to rush any decisions. After all, this job was providing for my family! How ironic would it be to mentor others on how to provide when I had no job! I smiled to myself; it was all so crazy. They (whoever "they" are) say you shouldn't make any significant changes in life for at least a year after a close family member or friend dies. For me, this was not a knee-jerk decision, rather a calling that I could not shake.

Just as I was processing all of these thoughts, the team trickled into the office. We greeted one another warmly. They were supportive and we shared hugs, laughs, and they even had my favorite tea drink from the best coffee shop in town. As I sipped on the warm drink I settled back more comfortably in the day. I was starting to appreciate how this job had served as a wonderful training grounds for leading the fellowship group. I needed to seek wisdom on my next steps as I considered this significant transition.

To help my consider this transition I set up a meeting with one of my mentors, Tim. We met at a local rooftop bar. We were only a few blocks from my office, yet the city looked so different from this perspective. It was an appropriate setting as I shared my new views on life and my work. This was the first time I was articulating the vision for the fellowship outside of my immediate family.

We were the only people sitting on the rooftop this particular morning, which fostered an intimate discussion about finances, faith, and how to grieve well. When I started to go into more details of my plan to leave work and focus on launching the fellowship, his eyes narrowed to focus on what I was saying. I could sense he, with his CFO background, was concerned about my plan. He actively listened before responding.

I felt more and more comfortable sharing my plans with him. When I was finally finished (I can be long-winded at times!), he responded. In a supportive manner, he looked at me and directly asked if I had prepared financially for such a bold decision. It was a great question, one that many friends and family members wouldn't have the boldness to ask. Did it take the wind out of my sails a little bit? Yes. But that is exactly why I consult guys like Tim on important matters before I act—I need a voice of caution sometimes.

Tim wasn't going to accept any surface-level answers. You really get to know someone when the conversation addresses how much money you have in the bank!

I thought back to how Pop had managed money. He and I would talk about budgeting often, and he gave me some of the most practical advice out of college. He encouraged me to spend twenty-five percent or less of my take home pay on housing. It was a lesson I took to heart and helped me develop a strong budgeting habit.

I refocused on the question at hand from Tim and told him that I had enough savings to last until the end of the year before needing to dip into investments and retirement funds. The clock was ticking. I told Tim that my plan was to focus on launching the fellowship first and then pursue new work. The schedule was: start the fellowship group in the fall and then prayerfully pursue a new career that challenged me to become a provider in a new way. I was feeding off of the energy and calling to launch the fellowship.

Though my heart wasn't into what my next career or job would be, I needed this warning to preparedness in order to honor those who depended on me.

I was fortunate to be in a position to take this time off. In a way it was a sabbatical season of life. After explaining this plan (if you can call it that—more like a hope and a prayer!), Tim relaxed his piercing eyes and seemed satisfied with my answer.

After a couple hours we wrapped up the conversation, prayed, and headed back to our respective work locations. It was just the conversation I needed at the time to get out my thoughts and feel how the felt aloud. I would soon be challenged with doubts and fears.

12

WHAT AM I DOING WITH MY LIFE?

I USED TO THINK I NEEDED TO SILENCE MY DOUBTS IN LIFE.
NOW I KNOW I NEED TO PRAY THROUGH MY DOUBTS.

After vocalizing my plan to Tim, I went back home and experienced a surprise ambush of doubt. Mental attacks of ineptitude and second-guessing blocked all the momentum I had felt earlier that very day with my mentor. Disparaging thoughts and negative self-talk filled my mind.

Was I really going to follow through with this crazy plan? More importantly, was I good enough to lead other men? Was I prepared to provide for not only my family but also people I had never met when I felt like I was still becoming a provider?

The questions continued to assail me one after another.

Did it really make sense to walk away from a job that I had invested heavily into with my MBA credentials? Would such a leadership role like that ever come up again?

My idyllic picture of launching the fellowship was beginning to face my real and growing inner doubts. Now that I had verbalized my plans out loud I was forced to really consider its consequences. I entered my office and submitted these questions as prayers. I shared some of these doubts with my wife. I leaned on my faith and family to restore confidence that yes, this transition was indeed a calling, not an overreaction to Pop's death.

The doubts came in strongly. It reminded me of Ephesians 6:13,16:

> Therefore, put on the full armor of God, so that when the day of evil comes, you may be able to stand your ground ... in addition to all of this, take up the shield of faith, with which you can extinguish all the flaming arrows of the evil one.[1]

I had survived the barrage of arrows attacking my desire and confidence by resting in my faith. By specifically turning each concern into a prayer, I was submitting to my Provider, my great Shepherd to bless and protect me. I was now ready to proceed. I needed this shield of faith for the challenges ahead.

————

"I don't mean to take over this meeting, but I'm about to do just that." I paused as I looked at my business partners. "I'm resigning as CEO."

It was our weekly leadership meeting time at the small tech company and I just unleashed the news. I was leaving to start the CL Thomas Fellowship program. My business partners stared back at me with a mixture of surprise and curiosity. The meeting room was heavy with silence.

For the last couple of months I had been back at the office after bereavement leave. Things were humming along near their regular cadence and pace but I knew I was being called to transition away. So after playing the conversation out in my head, I was finally experiencing the moment. I had finally told them. I was leaving.

When I returned to the office there had been so much excitement around sales that one team member exclaimed, "We all said, 'Justin would love this!'" I smiled and thought to myself, *This is an answer to prayer*. The sales pipeline had increased in my absence and it was just another confirmation that it was OK and even appropriate timing for me to transition out. The company would be just fine—stronger in fact in a number of ways. I could be free to fully explore the idea of launching the fellowship.

Everything with the transition plan went smoothly and I was even surprised when the founder of the company flew in from out of state to see me off on my final day. He was showing his full support in a way that I appreciated. What a gesture! I had the support of my wife, my soon-to-be former colleagues, and my mentors. I had no idea what the future would hold for me or the fellowship, but I was ready!

So here I was, having just resigned my position as CEO to focus on launching the fellowship. I couldn't imagine anything more important to do with my time than take a leap of faith into the unknown and start a nonprofit mentoring program around this theme of becoming a provider. However, some people were worried about me. Fortunately, I had addressed all their concerns through prayer and no matter what anyone said, I was committed to this work and plan. At the same time I don't want to discount the significance of this decision.

For me, this career change was a significant one. This may seem like a crazy bold decision to some and I'm not suggesting it to everyone. Yet the transition was the right move for me at the appropriate time. I felt I had given myself enough time and space to process.

It was time to develop the program and recruit guys into the first group.

———

And then … no one showed up.

It had been seven months since Pop's death. Fall was here and I wanted to launch.

Initially I thought, "This is going to be great. I've quit my job for this, it has to work out." Who wouldn't want to join this fellowship group! However I had a difficult time recruiting men into the program.

I could sense the arrows returning, the doubts creeping back into my mind. After several months of recruiting, fear started to swell in me. What kind of life calling is this? It would be embarrassing to fail to launch the fellowship.

I started this journey praying that the fellowship program would outlive me and provide for many lives. Now I was praying it wouldn't end before it even began! I had to keep practicing praying to remind myself to trust God; after all, God had given me the word *fellowship*, and so God had a plan with this adventure that was larger than mine.

In addition to fear about the fellowship, I still had no idea what I would do for my career next steps. I had no job, my runway was expiring, and I didn't have a single recruit for the CL Thomas Fellowship—the dream I believed God had given me with such clarity.

Surprisingly, my work in launching the fellowship helped point me to a new direction just when I needed it most.

13

HUMBLED (AGAIN) AND LIFTED UP

I USED TO THINK WORDS WERE CHEAP. NOW I KNOW THE
POWER OF AN ENCOURAGING WORD TO CHANGE THE COURSE
OF YOUR LIFE.

To help launch the men's fellowship group I wanted to make a video to recruit applicants. Tim graciously agreed to join the video shoot which proved to be a critical moment in my career transition. This is just how life works with God: when you least expect it, opportunity arises. During the B-roll, Tim shared his personal experience with health coaching and the value he received in completing a health coach training program. As the videographer captured B-roll footage, I was collecting inspiration for my next career.

I had never even heard of health coaching or integrated medicine. Without knowing it, I was beginning to prepare for a career transition into the health and wellness industry.

I was intrigued and scribbled down *health coaching, Duke Integrative Medicine*. I learned that this program taught skills around active listening, the art of reflecting during conversations, and presenting powerful questions. I believed these could all contribute to the men's fellowship group I was preparing to launch. I was so driven to make the fellowship special I wanted to add any personal credentials that I could to help bolster the fellowship to potential applicants.

At this point, I didn't even understand what health coaching was, but I applied and got accepted. Once again I had no idea what I was doing, just following sincere desires—but I would soon face some obstacles along the way and be humbled.

I went to pay for the program during the early bird discount period and discovered I was too late. The class was at capacity and no longer accepting students! How could this happen? I was not only expecting a slot, but a discount! I thought I would be a gift to the class based on my business management experience. Now they didn't want me. After getting so excited about this opportunity, the door seemed to have shut abruptly. The program didn't have a slot for me.

For the first time since being a college student, I had complete flexibility in my schedule and I wasn't sure exactly what to do with it. During my time as CEO, I learned in both sales and hiring that it pays to be *pleasantly persistent*. I implemented this strategy upon the staff at Duke Integrative Medicine for the health coaching training program. I contacted them weekly. The program manager would receive an e-mail or call from me asking for a slot and it was likely now or never for me to complete this training program.

Eventually, another student dropped and guess who was on top of the waitlist! I signed up immediately, this time as a grateful student versus an entitled former small-business CEO. This would not be the last time health coaching provided a humbling opportunity for my personal growth.

During the second semester of the training program I needed to start coaching actual clients. I could use these as credit hours towards my national board certification requirements. I offered free coaching and started to add clients. While this was rewarding work, I wasn't making money and I was running out of my end-of-year financial runway. Then another mentor spoke life into my career.

Tim and I had arranged a call. We didn't talk often so I wanted to get this conversation just right. My plan was to offer his employees free health coaching services. I thought giving away more free services would lead to paid engagements. I realize now this was a flawed plan! I was really operating out of fear of rejection, but I told myself, "With more references I can gain more credibility, which will attract paying clients."

Tim answered and I immediately went into my prepared sixty-second pitch. When I finished I remembered thinking, *I nailed it!* Then came his response.

"You have to provide for your family, right?" Naturally the word *provide* hit me in the gut with the strength of a heavyweight boxer.

"Well, yes," I said in response. Henry timed his comments perfectly. I had already achieved enough credit hours for certification. I just hadn't changed my pitch from *free* to *this is worth your investment.*

The light bulb went off. I realized I was operating out of fear, not as a confident provider. He asked how much my services cost and I made something up on the call.

He then said, "OK, I know what I am going to do." I had no idea what that meant but I thanked him anyway as I felt like I needed to bounce off the ropes from his jab—although helpful, the call stung.

The next day Tim posted a message on his personal LinkedIn account. It remains one of the most thoughtful things anyone has ever said about me. I read his message in surprise delight:

I love Justin. Super guy. Very intentional. Great heart.

Been a successful entrepreneur and then after an experience with coaching, decided to hang up a shingle as a coach.

He's just getting going and offering up really, really affordable rates and beard-growing tips. If I was 10 years younger I'd sign up in a heartbeat.

With that gift I got my first three paying clients! More importantly, I regained my confidence. The blessing of words of life spoken over me changed the trajectory of my career, the fellow-ship, and my provider journey.

For me, Tim's advice and referral was Proverbs 18:21 in action: "Death and life are in the power of the tongue." He believed in me and gave my vision life.

The power of mentors and direct feedback had blessed me again. Through yet another humbling experience I learned the need to ask for help. I also witnessed how my paid clients tended to be more responsive and committed in the process while my free clients struggled to maintain focus and honor our meeting times.

God taught me something else through this: Things matter to us when they cost us something. I would not have started the CL Thomas Fellowship if I didn't lose my father. The provider journey has cost me financial sacrifices and even more challenging, it has cost me my pride over and over. Leaving my title of CEO, trying something new with both the fellowship and health coaching and struggling to recruit participants into both groups exposed areas of weakness in my life that needed improvement to become a provider.

———

But back to my problem of not having any eager providers-in-training on board with my first fellowship experience.

When I didn't have any interest in the program after several months of recruiting, anxiety started to build. This burden was based in fear; my fear under the surface was that no one would show up. No one would show up to what I thought was one of my life's callings and my father's legacy.

Just as I persisted in contacting my health coaching program till I beat the door down, I had to persist at the doors of heaven—and watched a miracle unfold.

Through the seven months of planning and then recruiting, I kept praying the program would outlive me and provide for many lives. I prayed that the fellowship would create a positive ripple effect for many generations. I had to keep practicing prayer to remind myself to trust God; after all, God had given me the term *fellowship*, and so God had a plan with this adventure that was larger than mine.

Finally, the applicants started coming in with only two weeks before launch date! And the coolest part? *Exactly seven guys signed up.* Seven excellent referrals from personal and professional connections formed an outstanding group—perfectly representing those seven months of focused prayer and planning.

14

THE HARDEST PART

I USED TO THINK THE HARDEST PART WAS STARTING. NOW I
KNOW IT'S BEING THERE IN THE THIRD QUARTER.

I looked down at my watch—7:30 p.m. I looked back up to
see four men staring at me and there should have been
seven. The guys knew what was coming next. Push-ups!

We were half way through the inaugural CL Thomas Fellowship. I had successfully recruited seven men into the group and
up until this point we had perfect attendance and started out so
strong. I had a motivated, smart, and eager group of men in the
fellowship. We had been reading books, memorizing scripture,
having lunch and learn sessions with my mentors and taking on
personal challenges to help us all become providers. However we
had some missing in action this month and not just one or two by
three! For most groups this is no big deal—but those groups are
not the CL Thomas Fellowship.

Part of the fellowship experience is signing a covenant to be
present at the meetings unless providentially hindered. I know
this may sound intense, and it is. It's a test to see how the men
honor their commitments. Things will come up in life. That is
exactly what happened to a few of the fellowship guys this night.
They had real challenges ranging from car issues to work responsibilities; yet the covenant was still broken. When covenants are

broken, so is trust and there needs to be amends made. We pay our debt in the fellowship through push-ups.

After completing my health coaching certification I wanted to explore ways of integrating a physical fitness component to the fellowship experience. Push-ups seemed to be a good idea!

I was starting to appreciate how being physically fit not only allows us to fulfill our chores, it is a provider habit that enables us to protect others. Think back to the image of a shepherd guarding and comforting his sheep in Psalm 23. It's hard to feel comfort unless you feel safe. I always felt safe around Pop.

Being a safe and strong provider goes beyond the strength to physically protect your family or friend in a fight. That moment may come occasionally, but the moment that is guaranteed to present itself weekly or even daily are the mundane physical needs of your life. We don't appreciate how fortunate most of us are to have healthy bodies capable of blessing and protecting those in our life. Whether it's holding a baby for hours, chopping wood, or simply changing a light bulb, you need to be physically engaged and not resting on the couch all day.

It's amazing how physical fitness is tied directly to our mental state. By reading books and memorizing Scripture, we are building mental strength—mental toughness, if you will. We need to build physical strength to fuel the mental toughness, and to be ready for the physical defense for our families and potential victims across our paths.

Let's not discount our health anymore. In fact, Scripture tells us in I Corinthians 6:19-20,

> Do you not know that your bodies are temples of the Holy Spirit, who is in you, whom you have received from God? You are not your own; you were bought at a price. Therefore honor God with your bodies.

It's plain and simple. We have one body. It's not even really ours. We were given this by God and we have the opportunity to honor God with them. And we haven't even talked about the great side effects of being physically fit with more productive work outcomes.

The guys were not considering all of this when I told them to grab a spot on the carpet and get in the push-up position. They groaned at what they knew was coming. Amends needed to be paid before we could discuss the provider theme of the night.

I counted out twenty-five reps, then we paused to recover before completing another twenty-five pushups. The room was silent, just the heavy breathing that comes from abrupt and unexpected exercise. The men had come for tea and a comfortable seat on my sofa to explore our book and theme. Comfort could wait as we had twenty-five final push-ups to complete.

"Guys, we are entering the third quarter," I said as we settled into my office together after completing the seventy-five push-ups. "Just like in a race or game, this is the hardest part. We've completed half of the fellowship and there is more to go. The first quarter of any new activity or commitment like this tends to be exciting. You start with all the promise and possibility of an unknown adventure. The second quarter of that journey allows you to settle in and create some group norms. The third quarter, where we are now, is what gets most of us. It's easy to become tired from the first half of the journey. You look ahead but can't see the end in sight yet. You have to make a choice if it's worth continuing on. You just need to get through this third quarter so that you make it to the further quarter where adrenaline takes over and the end in site. What are we going to do?"

Of course I was saying this to the guys that made it to the meeting, and I would soon share a similar message to the men who were not present. It's important as a leader to demonstrate you have standards and to address things immediately. If the standards are not being met people need to know. This is both a leadership challenge and a provider challenge. We all have to find our own authentic style of blessing and protecting others. Push-ups was my strategy. Why push-ups? Seventy-five push-ups is no small feat after all. It's not because I want the most muscular group of men in my fellowship. It's because of what I've learned about the truth of being a provider. Providing requires presence and pain. I wanted to protect them from laziness, from not finishing strong. In this particular moment of the fellowship we were being tested with developing the provider character trait of "being there."

Retired Navy SEAL David Goggins put it best: "I don't stop when I'm tired. I stop when I'm done."[1] Similarly, the provider makes a covenant to show up and finish strong. The question is simple, yet difficult to keep: *Will you be there?* Being there means being fully present. It might look like being physically present such as the men in the fellowship showing up for our monthly meeting. It requires us to be disciplined with time management. It's demonstrating commitment and respect.

Being there signals to the other person you are choosing to spend your time with them and that they are worth it. This is how you form deep, meaningful relationships—push through the third quarter for the satisfaction of finishing your commitments.

15

BEING BROTHERS

I USED TO JUST WANT THE BENEFITS OF FELLOWSHIP. NOW I
KNOW THAT YOU NEED TO LET YOURSELF BE KNOWN IN ORDER
TO BENEFIT FROM FELLOWSHIP.

I remember pressing the phone against my red ear. I was nervous, face flush, waiting for the other end to pickup. I was in the 6th grade and was on the cusp of asking out my first girlfriend. I had no idea what that exactly meant but through social pressure and what I thought was true love, here I was. Risking it all, red faced, ready to ask this girl out. It was the classic "DTR" conversation—*defining the relationship.* Something in my sixth-grader soul wanted the benefits of having a girlfriend without really knowing what was required of me.

The call ended successfully, she said yes! Less than six months later we broke up.

I had no idea what I was supposed to do as a boyfriend and how I could possibly take a girl out without a car. The uncertainties of a middle school dating relationships is similar to most of our adult relationships. We don't know who our close friends are versus those that are just acquaintances. When we do have close friends we still haven't defined what that means and how to make them meaningful relationships that spur one another along. My relationship with my brother is a perfect example of the untapped potential of introducing more intentionality and purpose into relationships.

I had always gotten along with my brother and respected him, yet we had a surface-level relationship. We would see each other during the holidays and make occasional trips to visit. Once I made the commitment to become a provider I wanted more support, accountability, and clarity from my inner circle. The first step was just to identify my inner circle! I knew I wanted my wife and brother to be included, so I took a page from my sixth-grade experience and set up a call—except this time I was more confident in the "why" behind the ask. I organized a conference call between my brother and my wife, Amy. The conversation went something like this:

"John, I want you to know the purpose of doing this is so that I am a better husband, father, and man of God. If at any time you feel like I am missing the mark or not being completely transparent with you, call me out on that. And if that doesn't work you have my permission to talk with Amy." I then looked at my wife and gave her the same permission for John to hear.

"Amy, if you ever feel like I am not providing for you in Christlike fashion or you are worried about me being untruthful or unfaithful in any way, you have my permission to ask John about it directly."

This felt like a significant moment in my relationship with my brother and wife. I was inviting them in and exposing myself to them. For most of my life I had wanted the benefits of being in fellowship without the sacrifice it took. This intentional exercise was helping me to learn how to have genuine fellowship.

I scheduled monthly one-on-one time calls with my brother and we agreed on four categories to check in with one another to add purpose to our conversation:

- Financial Transparency
- Sexual Purity
- Relationship with God
- Family Leadership

During each call we would give each category a simple grade of Red/Yellow/Green to keep it simple and honest. We called it "Being Brothers" and it is a relationship I encourage the men in the fellowship to establish. It takes intentionality and can be a bit awkward, but what great things in life aren't uncomfortable at first? My experience with DTR conversations has helped me create much deeper relationships, something I tried doing back in sixth grade and am now just figuring out, one call at a time.

16

WEAKNESS EXPOSED

I USED TO THINK PHYSICAL FITNESS WAS JUST ABOUT PUSHING YOUR BODY. NOW I KNOW IT REQUIRES A VISION AND MENTAL TOUGHNESS.

I n order to experience personal growth, it's helpful to have a vision of your ideal future state while being brutally honest with where you are today. For instance, when you want to get out of debt, you first need to know how much debt you currently have so you can create a winning strategy. It sounds easy but we tend not to take time to come up with an authentic vision. I experienced a vision exercise that freaked me out and inspired me during my health coaching training course.

"Get into a comfortable position with both of your feet planted on the floor," the teacher instructed. I was sitting in a classroom with thirty-five fellow students at Duke Integrative Medicine. Classmates had flown in from all over the country and even as far as Brazil and Israel to attend our first week of an integrative health coaching training program. I was impressed with the diversity of the class, but I was beginning to feel slightly out of place—actually *really* out of place—with this meditation exercise. I wanted practical tips and how-to guides on facilitating group discussions for my upcoming fellowship groups. And honestly I wanted the credibility of saying I was certified at Duke. My internal dialogue was interrupted as my teacher instructions continued, "Allowing your eyes to close or cast down, begin to focus your awareness on your breath." Yup, I was now ready to leave. However, I stuck it out—after all, I had paid good money for this training and practically begged for the final slot!

The breathing exercise continued for another minute or two. When I was settling in, I heard further instructions, "Your future self is waiting for you; waiting to talk to you." I was definitely the skeptic in the room during this exercise. Then something incredible happened. I remember seeing a clear picture of my future self. What was going on! This is some weird health-coaching mojo.

The teacher wrapped up the exercise. "When you open your eyes, please remain silent, pick up your paper and crayons and begin drawing whatever you remember from this journey."

I did what I was instructed and started drawing the image I saw in my head. My future self was a Navy SEAL. I had no intention of really transitioning from my civilian life to a military career. Plus simulating drowning and lack of sleep are not my heart's top desires. However the image represented strength and confidence. My future self was better than I was at the moment. Willing and able to protect those around me from harm with bold words and actions. Not soft, not timid; yet still *tender* in strength. I couldn't believe the exercise prompted such a clear vision. I felt far from achieving this future self.

Motivated by this vision, I signed up for a GoRuck Tough challenge. It's a team-based endurance event lead by Navy SEALs and other types of Military Special Operations professionals. It's a twelve-hour overnight event for civilians to get a small glimpse into special ops training by carrying a backpack with thirty pounds of weight, food, water, and essentials. The military operations leader, known as *cadre,* also brings a plethora of extra weight that the team has to carry throughout the night such as sandbags, water jugs, and logs while completing specific assigned tasks. Did I mention you actually pay for this experience? Crazy, I know! On top of all this craziness there is no winner; it is a team event to survive the litany of exercises and "missions" that the cadre presents. At the end, everyone receives a patch to commemorate the experience. I've completed over a half dozen of these events and although I received a patch at each one, my contribution level has drastically varied.

During my first GoRuck Tough challenge I was scared to death. I had no idea what I was doing or really why I signed up. Even after my vision exercise I was insecure about what I could possibly contribute to this team event. Not a good start. The event started at nine p.m. and darkness surrounded me as I anxiously awaited starting instructions from the cadre along with my other teammates. Everyone was silent. I could feel the nervousness swell inside of me. I positioned myself at the back of the line as much as possible and didn't talk. In preparation for this twelve-hour challenge I bought an old hockey practice shirt to provide extra cushion underneath all my layers of clothing. Imagine an athletic short sleeve short but with shoulder and chest padding. I was worried about my body not being able to handle the load of the event. I thought this hack would work. It didn't.

The event started with some basic physical training drills. One of the drills was swinging your rucksack in front of you and as I was completing this exercise, I noticed something spewing out of my bag. My water bladder had sprung a leak with all the swinging! As I completed rep after I rep I viewed in terror as my life source, my packed water get less and less! Finally this torture finished when the final swing cadence call was yelled out and I could secure my remaining water. We then moved into team drills.

For one of the missions during my first GoRuck Challenge, the cadre pointed to me and said, "You are in charge." This was not my idea of fun. *Why did I do this again?* The cadre quickly explained that I needed to organize my team of twenty-plus men over an obstacle while only having three shoes touching the ground at any given time in a designated area. Now I became completely unraveled. I simply stood in silence. I froze. I was running the cadre's instructions through my head, hoping for a brilliant strategy to suddenly appear. I was nowhere close to my vision of a strong, capable leader who could be trusted. My team realized I was worthless and the mob mentality took over as they pushed past me and took turns shouting instructions one after another. Not surprisingly, we failed to complete the challenge and had to do some penalty exercises. I had failed.

I quickly returned to the comfort of the shadows. The event carried on and the cadre brought us to a spot with some "presents." This was no Christmas morning gift exchange. Instead I saw two massive logs and a "regular" log. The large ones required three to four guys to carry it on their shoulders and the regular one only required a couple guys. I hoped that I could contribute more as a team player rather than the leader. Not the vision I had of a Navy SEAL, but at least I was making attempts toward my vision. I started out under the big log thinking my hockey shirt was going to crush it. Nope. I got crushed.

Doing my best to go unnoticed, I started dropping the idea of achieving my Navy SEAL vision and shrank once again to the back of the line until I got out of the log carrying rotation. My shoulders were burning from pain. I couldn't imagine carrying those logs.

Over ten hours later we were still competing in the event. We had gone through the night, the sun was up and the end in sight. We had about a mile left to go and they needed a "casualty"—someone to play hurt and be carried to the finish line. As one of the smaller guys on the team, I gladly volunteered.

From this example, you can tell I was not in the mindset of blessing or protecting anyone other than myself. I was too fearful, too timid, and weak (mentally and physically) to contribute to the overall group. I tried to do my part, but I was exposed as a weak teammate. I was operating out of a selfish mentality—it was all about me. Even from the beginning I was focused on becoming the Navy SEAL future self to fulfill my vision, not once considering the needs around me.

We are not called to fade in the background just because it feels safe. I knew I could do better, be better. I vowed to never use that hockey shirt again and to get stronger for the next event.

17

WHAT I LEARNED THROUGH WASHING THE DISHES

I USED TO THINK THE STAGE WAS WHERE I NEEDED TO SHINE. NOW I KNOW THAT INTEGRITY IN THE MUNDANE IS TRUE WORTH.

The GoRuck event showed me how it's not about shining bright for a moment. I hadn't shone at all during my first couple of events! I kept trying to contribute in these crazy challenges but kept falling short, always at the rear of the pack. These endurance challenges required me to persevere through the night and its seemingly endless challenges. I realized it was not just physically challenge, but also required a great deal of mental fortitude, an area that I had not spent time working on. I needed to build myself up from the ground up physically and emotionally. It was time to take an honest look at my strengths and weaknesses.

First, I realized I was a big fish in a small pond. I grew up attending a small Christian school where leadership positions were offered to everyone. I was Romeo in the school play, president of my class, and captain of the basketball team. I attended a small liberal arts college which also afforded plenty of opportunities. I was elected president of my business fraternity as only a sophomore and later served as large group coordinator for the student Christian group. All of these positions put me "on stage" and in front of people.

As life progressed, I continued to find myself being the face of organizations and teams. My first job out of college was training physicians and hospital staff members. Later, during my MBA program I looked forward to presentations so much that I made side bets with one of my classmates that I could take whatever word or phrase he gave me just minutes before my presentation and incorporate it in seamlessly. One time he gave me the word "angels" which was challenging but I made it into the presentation: "This is a proven process and when we implement and experience how smoothly the supply chain functions, it will feel as if angels are singing, the new process will bring peace of mind to management." Like I said, I lived for the stage.

I have to admit, this is where my father and I differed. He knew true character is built on integrity. He knew *integrity* was quiet and authentic and hates the spotlight. He showed me it was developed off the grid.

However, I have had to learn the value of integrity the hard way. Having sustained experience of being in front of people, whether facilitating meetings or formally presenting, developed some positive characteristics but they also had some unintentional consequences, specifically in my job priorities. I started to discount experiences that did not help me get recognition. I would work tirelessly on "spotlight" activities such as presentations, speeches, and planning big events. However, the motivation to do the mundane or background work never made it on my priority list. This was why I struggled so mightily during endurance events; I struggled to just labor on when commitment in the mundane was required for success.

I was washing the dishes one night when this lesson of honoring the behind-the-scenes moments of life finally hit me. Ever since I heard that word "fellowship" from God, I've tried to tune into and become more sensitive to these gentle nudges from God. Rather than focusing my thoughts on how to be "the guy," I needed to serve more and not just serve but to serve *joyfully*. I realized that every night I have an opportunity to do the dishes for our family. It was an opportunity to demonstrate "GoRuck mental toughness" in doing something I didn't necessarily want to do, but that it could help me *develop the habit* of joyfully serving others and persevering when no one was looking. That's integrity. There would be no prize or celebration of my achievement. Yet this was important work that I felt God was calling me to do-washing dishes.

I also realized that I didn't require a date night with my wife to connect or have fun. I could have valuable time with her by serving her, washing the dishes and engaging her in thoughtful conversation. We still do date nights, don't get me wrong, I just needed to start seeing all the opportunities of life to serve her and our family well.

I was trying to exorcise my demons of desiring the spotlight one dish at a time. As each dish got washed I was making progress. My mental challenge was to put the same effort into cleaning up as I did on polishing that perfect pitch. The challenge was real. I did not start with the right attitude, but at least I started. Eventually my attitude caught up to my behavior. For once I was truly serving with a joyful heart—all thanks to some dishes. Without realizing it, I was becoming stronger for my next GoRuck challenge through this basic task.

In *The Four Loves*, CS Lewis talks about not only imitating Christ at Calvary but also imitating in Christ in the everyday busyness of life.

> Our model is the Jesus, not only of Calvary, but of the workshop, the roads, the crowds, the clamorous demands and surly oppositions, the lack of all peace and privacy, the interruptions. For this, so strangely unlike anything we can attribute to the Divine Life in itself, is apparently not only like, but is the Divine life operating under human conditions.[1]

I now aspire to imitate Christ in the mundane, everyday moments. One dish at a time.

18

STRENGTH DISCOVERED

I USED TO THINK GENEROSITY WAS JUST ABOUT GIVING EXTRA
MONEY. I NOW KNOW I'VE BEEN CALLED TO GIVE OF MYSELF
TILL IT HURTS.

At the end of the first class of the CL Thomas Fellowship, I had a special surprise for the fellows. Instead of meeting in the living room or my office as usual, I invited them outside to the fire pit. We had endured nine months of rigorous assignments. They thought the new meeting location was the surprise and we started as normal reciting our memory verses.

Then instead of continuing on with our standard fellowship meeting agenda I paused and told them I had a gift for them.

I lifted a large box onto the table and told them the story of another GoRuck challenge. This time one with a very different ending to my first experience.

I told the guys in the fellowship that I wanted to share my provider story through my experience with GoRuck challenges. Just as I shared with you, I described my first few failures during these events. Apparently it had been just long enough to forget the pain and frustration so I signed up for another beatdown. After I signed up for this particular event I realized I had a scheduling conflict. My wife was going to be out of town for a weekend conference. I needed someone to watch my two daughters while I completed the overnight challenge. Pop and Mom had scheduled to come down to to watch the kids to fill in the gaps.

And then Pop passed away. His death came just a few weeks before my event. I wasn't sure if Mom still wanted to come down or not. I wasn't sure if I even wanted to participate, but Mom assured me she was looking forward to spending time with her grandchildren. It was the first time we had scheduled a family memory expecting Pop to be there and he wasn't. This was a bitter reminder of how we were forced to go on with life without Pop. New memories would be made without him and that realization was still hard to grasp.

I shared with the guys in the fellowship that during this particular event I found myself comparing my physical pain with what Pop might have felt during his heart attack. I would try to draw strength as my shoulders bruised under the heavy weight of the logs or as my forearm skin chafed against metal weights. At least I was living. At least I could carry on.

The event was just like my first one in many ways. It had the same weight requirement, time duration, and rules. However, this experience would be far different as I carried in a provider mindset from start to finish. I needed to prove to myself I was a changed man, or at least a *changing* man.

During this particular challenge, I went from a silent participant to a more confident and engaged one, encouraging on teammates sharing tips on strategy for carrying logs and sandbags. I was taking lessons from the dishes and serving others, anyway I could. When a team leader needed an assistant he chose me, someone he could trust to do whatever needed to be done. Then near the end of the grueling twelve-hour event our cadre made the dreaded announcement as he pointed to one of my teammates: "Everyone, stop. You" —pointing to a teammate—"are a casualty, and someone needs to carry you to the finish line."

The group stopped, exhausted. Everyone took a moment to catch our breath and soak in this new challenge from the cadre. We were all exhausted. Feet blistered, shoulders chaffed, and the heat of the morning starting to increase. Someone needed to carry this teammate. The bar had been raised.

To their surprise—and my own—I stepped up and slung the guy across my shoulders and walked onward. No words spoken, just action taken. When I didn't think I had anything to give, I reached deeper.

That is the provider mentality. I didn't get there the first time. I wanted to be carried by someone else during my first challenge. Now here I was lifting the load so we could press on towards our goal as a team to completion.

I should mention that I'm just an average guy. I reach five feet ten inches if I have the right shoes on. I weigh 155 pounds with the right clothes. I am not the Incredible Hulk, I'm just a regular guy. And I picked up that teammate and carried him as far as I could. My action inspired the rest of the team and they followed me and then others took turns carrying our fallen comrade.

After we crossed the finish line and received our event patch, one of my teammates came straight over to me with intensity in his eyes. He was still riding high on adrenaline from the event and the thrill of being done—finally! He put his arm around me and said, "Dude, you are a badass. You're skinny but strong. I couldn't believe you picked up that guy."

Let me tell you, it is so much more rewarding being strong enough to carry someone else (and being called a badass was kind of cool, I will admit). It took time, training, and a change in attitude.

———

After I finished sharing this story with the fellowship guys I started to open the box I had set before them. It had the word "GoRuck" on it. I told them that similar to my experience doing GoRuck challenges, we are all being challenged with opportunities to provide for others. The question is are you preparing to be the one to carry someone when they need you to shoulder their burdens? Are you working on developing your strengths for the benefit of others? Or are you happy collecting "badges" in life just for your own glory?

I told the men I wanted to give them their own GoRuck rucksack. It represented my personal journey of moving from selfishness and weakness to strength that comes from providing for others by serving them. I wanted to give them my best during the fellowship and more importantly I wanted to equip them to become providers. The bag equipped them to take on the mantle of being a provider out into the field. I called up each guy individually and spoke a quick work of encouragement and blessing over them as I gave each their own bag. Even more special was that each bag had a custom patch attached to the bag with the CL Thomas Fellowship logo to commemorate their accomplishment of completing the program.

We huddled around the fire pit as the night closed in, reflecting on the journey together. I knew it was a special moment, and I just soaked it all in. We all had further to go to become the provider God wanted us to, but I was confident the fellowship had helped us all start the journey with a new passion and intentionality that did not previously exist in our lives. The vision of the fellowship had become a reality.

I'm glad I listened to that voice in the shower that dropped the word "fellowship" seemingly out of nowhere. I needed to grow in my role as a provider on short notice for my family. I love sharing everything I have to the men of the fellowship. The best of Pop's life lessons, the Scriptures that challenge my thinking, the mentors who shaped my career, and my resources to help the men experience biblical generosity. The great part is that it's not just *my* calling. We are all invited to this provider adventure.

The GoRuck challenge is an event. There are lots of great lessons to be learned during the event, but it always ends. The journey of being a provider is a grand adventure that never ends. Being a provider is a weighty call throughout a lifetime. You can develop into a trusted provider who is equipped to bless and protect others. Someone who makes a positive difference, and builds people up. In the next section I will present two simple visual frameworks—the Bless and Protect Matrix and the Provider Wheel—which encapsulate how to become a provider with a biblical perspective.

Don't lag in the back of the pack hoping to be carried through life. Get in the game—join the invitation to grow your provider muscles. It may hurt like those logs but you will be ready to lift up others when it's time.

19

BLESS & PROTECT MATRIX

A fter my own self-experimentation to become a provider and launching the CL Thomas Fellowship, I wanted to codify the lessons for others to enjoy the same personal growth. I had learned from Pop's letter and Psalm 23 that being a provider meant blessing and protecting others, as Jesus does for us. I asked myself: *If Jesus's provision is to bless and protect us, what does that look like in our lives?* I then did what many MBA grads would do in this scenario—create a classic 2x2 matrix! This helped me explore the two key dimensions of providing for others through blessing and protecting. The matrix challenged me to evaluate which quadrants I naturally fell into as well as the opportunity for growth.

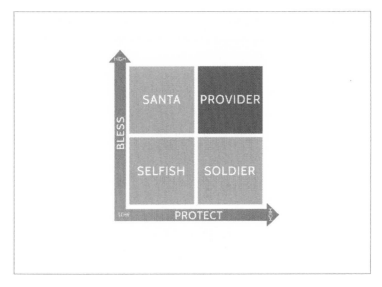

Figure 1: The Bless & Protect Matrix

The Four Quadrants

- ***Upper Left: Santa.*** Santa represents someone who is
  generous and loving but lacks the guiding hand of a
  protector. They love to bless people with gifts, yet they
  disregard the need to ever speak hard truth in one's life.
  They default to solving problems and burdens through
  gifts, which certainly blesses others, but it does not fully
  satisfy the need. The Santa quadrant allows you to stay
  in the safe space of giving more and more and receiving
  praise for your apparent generosity. It's a fun quadrant
  to be in, both for the giver and receiver, yet there is a
  deeper version of providing.
- **Lower Left: Selfish.** Unlike Santa, this quadrant is not
  externally facing with its low levels of both blessing and
  protecting characteristic traits. Individuals here are in
  survival mode. They are doing the best they can and

simply feel there is no excess time, energy, or resources for anyone outside of themselves. This mindset is a self-fulfilling prophecy and results in an inability to help others. They might want to help others, they just don't believe they can bless or protect others in this moment.

- *Lower Right: Soldier.* This quadrant is high on the protect trait, but low on the bless trait. A "soldier" represents someone who is strong and reliable but lacks the softer, blessing characteristics. On the one hand, people may feel safe around "soldiers," but hesitant to be vulnerable and open to such a harsh figure.

- *Upper Right: Provider.* A well developed individual has become a provider when they possess both a high degree of blessing and protecting characteristics. This is the ideal quadrant to grow into and maintain. It is the most challenging and risky of all quadrants. You must simultaneously exhibit "soft" and "hard" personalities, from tenderness to brute strength. This does not come naturally and requires a variety of character strengths to model the Shepherd figure of Psalm 23.

————

After reviewing the Bless & Protect Matrix, I asked myself, "What specific traits did Pop use to bless and protect others?" How did he get to the provider quadrant and what does Scripture say about the ideal provider? The 2x2 matrix was a great start but I wanted more clarity. This Provider Wheel helped me take the necessary next steps in my provider journey.

20

THE PROVIDER WHEEL

I returned to my notes that I had drawn on Pop's easel. I reviewed those traits again and categorized them all in a wheel to reflect how all the spokes needed to extend in strength to help build momentum along our provider journey.

Before I go into the provider wheel I want to acknowledge that becoming a provider is tough.

It's far easier to live a life receiving from others and blending into the background. Even after you have reviewed the Provider Wheel, stepping into the Provider role has its challenges. Let's face some of these head on. Here are the top five excuses that I personally uttered along my journey and those that I hear from others on why they do not believe they can become a provider:

1. **I need to focus on me first before providing.** This sound reasonable and even admirable on the surface. However this limiting belief claims that God has not been generous enough to you, therefore you can't provide until more work is done. The work has already been done, you just need to give in whatever measure has been given to you. It's like the guys who say "I need to get in shape before I go to the gym." The problem is

you likely are not going to push yourself as much on your own as you would in a group workout or gym setting that offers more relational support. This concept works the same with becoming a provider. You become a better provider by providing. Yes, it is true we may not be a seasoned provider, but we can still provide something to someone. I believe we can all provide for someone no matter what life stage we are in.

2. **I don't have a lot of money so I can't provide.** This sells the word provider so short it's painful to hear. Don't think of "provider" as the 1950s Dad figure bringing home a paycheck as the pinnacle of providing. Our baseline definition needs to change from bringing in the money to blessing and protecting. You know that now, yet it bears repeating so it stays with you: Providing = Blessing + Protecting. Out of the 8 provider characteristics (which we'll get to in a moment) only 2 deal with finances. There are many more opportunities to bless and protect others beyond finances.

3. **I don't have a spouse/kids so I don't need to be a "provider" yet.** Have you ever needed a blessing or some protection in your life? I'm sure you have regardless of your marital status! Why do we believe the lie that providing then is only for our spouse or kids. We absolutely want and will provide for our family when the time comes. There are many others that God has put in our life to bless and protect. Plus, if you are single, don't you want some practice before you lead a family?

4. **I'm not (spiritually/emotionally) mature enough to be a provider.** Similar to excuse #1, in order to grow and mature you need to engage. Doing nothing is not going to build confidence or belief that you are ready to provide. We need to resist the lie that "when I feel more mature, I can provide more." It's similar to sports. You

don't just wait around until you have matured into an All-Star to start playing the game. You put in the work and build the skills to become the best version of yourself. We all start out as a "rookie" provider, and we all have the opportunity to become a seasoned "veteran" provider that allows us to have more influence in our spheres of influence.

5. **I don't have a good example to follow.** One of the CL Thomas fellows remarked that there were very few examples of providers in today's church. He said "Yes, Jesus is an example of doing all of these perfectly, but there are not many men leading lives in this manner." Others state that they simply hadn't seen a solid provider (physically, emotionally, spiritually, financially, etc) in life. This is a real barrier to overcome for a lot of people as it is a struggle to replicate something you haven't seen or experienced. I hope this book provides the example that has been missing in your life.

How to Use the Provider Wheel

So what helped me go from believing those excuses to overcoming them? The Provider Wheel gave me a visual guide for how I can practically bless and protect others. I typically start my day by praying for one person to bless and protect that day. When I'm not sure what to do for them I refer to the Provider Wheel for ideas. It's that simple. You can't become someone new unless you try to do new things. You need to change your mindset from default position of focusing on you to serving others. It's not easy but it is worth the effort. God made us not to glorify ourselves but to glorify Him. We do that by loving others, by blessing and protecting them in real, practical ways that are found on the Provider Wheel below.

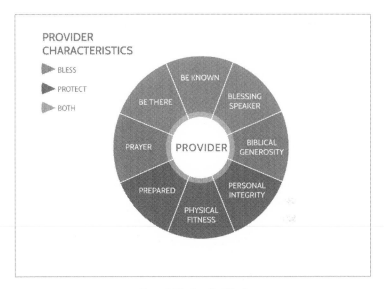

Figure 2. The Provider Wheel

Provider Wheel Summary

The wheel presents the eight characteristic traits that helps us become a provider. It is color coded with orange representing blessing traits, blue for protecting traits, and brown for traits that overlap both. I created this out of a personal need to have a comprehensive plan to guide me, yet something that I could make personal and adapt to my future provider opportunities. Below is a summary of the eight areas to develop in your life to become a provider.

Blessing Traits (top, orange)

- **Be There**: blessing others with true attention and care
- **Be Known**: blessing others by sharing our story and learning theirs-giving the gift of being heard

- **Blessing Speaker**: blessing others through our intentional words

Protecting Traits (bottom, blue)

- **Prepared**: protecting others through wise planning
- **Physical Fitness**: protecting others by being healthy and strong
- **Personal Integrity**: protecting others with honesty, serving them with holiness

Overlap Traits (middle, brown)

- **Prayer**: going to the ultimate Provider for strength and wisdom; blessing and protecting others through petitions
- **Biblical Generosity**: blessing and protecting others through giving of ourselves to meet the needs of others

During the fellowship we spend one month on each Provider Wheel trait to ensure we are addressing all of the provider characteristics. We encourage one another to grow in these areas and develop new healthy habits to increase our bless and protect muscles. The curriculum is constantly evolving but in general each month we read a book, memorize scripture, and have a specific challenge related to an area of the provider wheel. You can view resources (including a color version of the Matrix and Wheel) online all for free at www.clthomasfellowship.org.

21

WHO TO PROVIDE FOR?

N ow that you are armed with the Bless and Protect Matrix and Provider Wheel, you are hopefully feeling more equipped to start providing. You can start on your own or in a group, however there is a fundamental question we need to address. *Who* are we supposed to provide for in life? That seems like the logical next question to ask. Here is the good news: Jesus provides us a guiding light through a story you are likely familiar with in Luke 10. We gain clarity on who to provide for in the parable of the Good Samaritan.

We are like the man who asked Jesus in Luke 10:25, "What must I do to inherit eternal life?" He was seeking validation for what he was already doing. Similarly, we are asking, "In order to feel I have become a provider, what must I do and whom should I provide for?" I bet you are already putting forth effort in providing for those in your life. It's natural to seek justification on the hard work we do.

Jesus asks the man in Luke 10:26-28, "What is written in the Law? How do you read it?"

The man confidently answers, "Love the Lord your God with all your heart and with all your soul and with all your strength and with all your mind, and love your neighbor as yourself."

Jesus smiles and responds, "You have answered correctly. Do this and you will live."

The man presses Jesus again for further clarification and focuses on the thorny issue at hand. It's easy to love God. He is perfect after all. But loving our neighbor is more challenging. Luke 10:29 captures the man's internal dilemma, "And who is my neighbor?"

We face a similar challenge. We want to be providers who honor God, but in order to be an effective provider we need to know who counts as someone I should provide for, or *who is my neighbor*?

Thankfully Jesus answers the question of who we should help in an unexpected way by telling a parable. Through the parable we learn how a priest and a Levite—holy men—pass by a beaten man without assisting. The Samaritan does the opposite and *cares for the beaten man*. Jesus delivers the dagger at the conclusion of the parable when he turns to the man and asks, "Which of these three do you think was a neighbor to the man who fell into the hands of robbers." The man with all the answers responds that of course it is the Samaritan, to which Jesus replies "Go and do likewise."[1]

We are not to debate and analyze which neighbor or individual to provide for, we are called to provide for those in need. So while the question *who should I provide for?* is a reasonable question, the better question is *are we "doing likewise"*? Meaning, are we being the provider when we need to be?

Next we need to shift our focus away from "who" and focus on "when" to provide, given that we know we are called to provide for *anyone in our path*. Once again, we find the answer in scripture.

22

WHEN TO PROVIDE?

he previous chapter may have just overwhelmed you. I just suggested that *everyone* is a candidate for us to provide for, not just our family, anyone on our path like the Good Samaritan parable. So then, how is it humanly possible to provide for the needs all around us? I have personally felt overwhelmed at times just trying to figure out my personal career and feeling like a failure providing for my family. I get it.

Fortunately, Scripture provides wisdom in how we can discern a genuine need versus when our help is not needed. Remember there are two equal components to providing: blessing and protecting. You are not expected to bless everyone all the time. There is wisdom in knowing how to concurrently protect others (and yourself!) as part of providing. Galatians 6:2-5 provides a beautiful and practical roadmap for knowing when you need to bless someone and when you need to protect them:

> Carry each other's burdens, and in this way you will fulfill the law of Christ. If anyone thinks they are something when they are not, they deceive themselves. Each one should test their own actions. Then they can take pride in themselves alone, without comparing

themselves to someone else, for each one should carry their own load.[1]

What this passage tells us is that we are called to bless people when they have a burden but we are to protect people by not providing for small loads.

In the book *Boundaries,* Dr. Henry Cloud and Dr. John Townsend eloquently describe the difference between a burden and a daily load:

> The Greek words for burden and load give us insight into the meaning of these texts. The Greek word for burden means "excess burdens," or burdens that are so heavy that they weigh us down. These burdens are like boulders. They can crush us. We shouldn't be expected to carry a boulder by ourselves! It would break our backs. We need help with the boulders—those times of crisis and tragedy in our lives.
>
> In contrast, the Greek word for load means "cargo," or "the burden of daily toil." This word describes the everyday things we all need to do. These loads are like knapsacks. Knapsacks are possible to carry. We are expected to carry our own. We are expected to deal with our own feelings, attitudes, and behaviors, as well as the responsibilities God has given to each one of us, even though it takes effort.[2]

To become providers we need to be wise in discerning when to bless others and when to protect them. Galatians 6 provides an excellent resource in calling us to give ourselves sacrificially yet with wisdom. Becoming a provider requires some level of King Solomon wisdom of Proverbs—which my father meditated on daily—or we may do more harm than good. We need to discern and act.

Yet James in the New Testament encourages us not to get bogged down in waiting. We need to act to truly become providers:

Don't fool yourself into thinking that you are a listener when you are anything but, letting the Word go in one ear and out the other. Act on what you hear! Those who hear and don't act are like those who glance in the mirror, walk away, and two minutes later have no idea who they are, what they look like.

But whoever catches a glimpse of the revealed counsel of God —the free life!—even out of the corner of his eye, and sticks with it, is no distracted scatterbrain but a man or woman of action. That person will find delight and affirmation in the action.[3]

Let's explore how this all works in real life. How can we use the Bless and Protect Matrix and Provider Wheel in real life, all with a Solomon style of wisdom that helps move boulders? This is what I set out to explore and test one day, unannounced and awkwardly—but with zest. If all else fails, just try to have an *authentic eagerness* to bless and protect others.

23

WENDY

I USED TO THINK GOOD INTENTIONS WERE ENOUGH. I NOW
KNOW YOU NEED INTEGRITY TO TURN INTENTIONS INTO
POSITIVE ACTION.

Y ou can become a better provider and enjoy the life God
intended if you are willing to give of yourself until it
hurts or embarrasses you. Here is how I experienced
both emotions along my provider journey when trying to put the
Bless and Protect Matrix and Provider Wheel into action.

Before Pop passed away, my wife and I moved to the historic
town of Hillsborough, NC. Pop was able to visit our new home
shortly after our move, which is a fond memory of mine. During
his trip he asked how we liked the area and I told him I was
getting involved in the community by starting a new F3 workout
in downtown. F3 is an established community and there were
workouts around my new hometown but nothing in it at the time.
F3 describes themselves as a "national network of free, peer-led
workouts for men. We plant, grow, and serve these groups to
invigorate male community leadership[1]."

Pop asked what F3 stood for and I told him it was for fitness,
fellowship, and faith. I was part of the team that helped to establish and organize three workouts a week, and a monthly happy
hour for the fellowship. However, we weren't doing anything
around the third *F*, the faith component. I continued being very
involved in F3, not really thinking about that third *F* until Pop

passed and I came across a convicting scripture. James 1:27 reads:

> "Pure and genuine religion in the sight of God the Father means caring for orphans and widows in their distress and refusing to let the world corrupt you."[2]

My heart broke as I realized my mom was now a widow. This passage in James motivated me to think of other people in need, specifically widows who didn't have anyone in their lives to support them and who may need practical help. I had an idea.

At the next monthly F3 social I brought up the concept of "adopting a widow" as part of our faith work in F3. We would serve a widow and help with whatever she needed. After all, we were men who were waking up early and working out at least three times a week. We were all in decent shape (or at least had a desire to get there!) and this seemed to fit the intent of what F3 is all about. There was agreement amongst the group to give this idea a shot, so then we just needed to find a widow.

I asked the men to send me recommendations and even e-mailed a couple local pastors. Nothing. I personally didn't know of any widows in my neighborhood, and apparently I was not alone. I had no leads after this "brilliant idea" until I met the "poodle-walkin' guy."

One morning I decided to ruck (i.e. walk while wearing a weighted backpack) to and from the workout. I had just finished the workout and was walking back to my house, sporting a sweat-drenched outfit and a shovel flag. At every F3 workout site there is a flag attached to a shovel to indicate the starting point. Basically I looked like a tired, disheveled homeless guy walking the streets with a flag. As you might imagine this conjures some questions from onlookers (and some friendly horn honks) when I'm walking around like this. As I rucked back home I saw a man walking his dog towards me. "What's your mission?" the man stopped and asked me, looking inquisitively at the flag.

I told the gentleman that I was part of a free men's workout group. Then I noticed he was wearing a t-shirt from a local church. It reminded me of James 1:27 and I told him about our "adopt a widow" idea. I mentioned we were looking for someone to serve in our area and asked if he knew of anyone. His eyes brightened up and he told me he had just serviced a lady's home in town for work that might be in need. I immediately took out my phone and asked for his contact information. Right there on the spot I sent him an e-mail and signed it "workout guy Justin" so that he could remember me and and possibly share my contact information with the lady he had in mind. I got a much different response and received the following e-mail:

Hello Justin.

A pleasure meeting you this morning! Wendy is the lady I met this week through work.

She resides in an early 1990s-model doublewide. The yard needed some attention/maintenance and her crawlspace needed work to keep out creatures.

She expressed to me her financial woes due to poor health and extreme prescription drug cost.

She would probably be receptive to your mission.

Have a great day!

—Poodle-walkin' guy

He also provided me all of this lady's contact information from his work database! I don't want to get this guy fired so I'm trying to keep details of his profession limited. My poodle-walkin' friend probably violated a dozen or so client confidentiality policies. However, I was glad he took a risk and sent me Wendy's information! I had a lead. It felt like all of this was a divine meeting!

Then I did nothing.

A week or so later I was sitting in my home office. I had an afternoon free of any client calls or pressing deadlines. Then I thought of Wendy. I wanted to make sure this idea didn't continue to get lost in the noise of my life. I recognized that I wasn't taking action even though it was time. At that moment, for some reason I thought the best and most practical thing to do was to drive to Wendy's house unannounced. I was afraid that I might lose motivation if I waited any longer and that Wendy wouldn't answer her phone or e-mail from a stranger. (Why I thought she would answer the door from a stranger is beyond me!) I simply believed that I would have a better chance meeting her in person.

I walked out of my home office and into the kitchen where my wife was preparing lunch for our two young girls. I matter-of-factly asked her if I should wear a suit and tie since I was going to a lady's house unannounced. She naturally wanted more details regarding this idea.

Amy looked and emphatically stated that I would look like a cheesy salesman if I changed into a suit and went knocking on strangers' doors. She also said it was ridiculous that I was driving and not emailing or texting first. Fair point. Yet I was undeterred and full of zest. I loaded up in my car, still wearing my casual t-shirt and shorts from a work-from-home professional wardrobe, and started driving to Wendy's house.

Fifteen minutes later the GPS announced I had arrived. I was in the middle of a trailer park area but I didn't see the house number I was looking for. I drove up and down, scouring the homes but no luck finding Wendy's number. I then decided that I would go to the house closest to the GPS marker. It did not look welcoming. In fact, it was the worst home in the lot. I drove past the "Do Not Trespass" signs and walked up the driveway. The steps and porch had lumber littered all on it. There were multiple cars broken down in the front lawn and a no-soliciting sign on the door. Basically a lot of signs telling me to stop, abort mission! Naturally I pressed on.

I balanced my feet on the uneven stacked lumber on the front porch and knocked. No one came to the door. I started to feel this plan might have some strategic holes in it. Before I risked any getting any trespassing charges levied against me, I left and headed quickly back to my car. Perhaps my wife was right, I may need to try calling Wendy.

Wendy's number went to voicemail and I proceeded to rambled on about who I was, what F3 was, our desire to help out and to call back—who knows what else. When I finished the message I didn't feel confident she would return my call.

I didn't want to give up.

I then decided on a new strategy. I would drive to a more welcoming home, one without a "No Trespassing" sign and debris littering the entrance to ask if they knew Wendy! I located said house and started driving into the new driveway. Just as I pulled in there was a car exiting the driveway and a lady walking in front of the car. I pulled over to allow space for the car and pedestrian and then jumped out.

"Do you know Wendy?" I asked her.

"I'm Wendy," she replied.

"Great! I just left you a message."

The car paused beside us. The driver was an older gentleman and he (rightfully) looked suspiciously at me. Though I hadn't explained who I was or what I was doing, Wendy waved him on and said, "It's fine, you can go."

I thought this was strange, but the guy just did what Wendy said and drove right on by me!

I went on to explain to Wendy that someone recommended me to her as I was organizing a service project with my local workout group to serve a neighbor. She looked surprised and said, "Oh, I thought you were with the roofing company to fix my roof." I laughed and told her I couldn't do that, but that we could help with something else!

Fortunately Wendy did not call the cops on me and we spent the next twenty minutes talking.

It was the beginning of a friendship. In our short introductory conversation together, I learned that Wendy had been the caretaker for her parents and then for a friend with dementia. Over the past three years they had all died and she had accumulated a lot of their material goods, but didn't have the time or energy to organize it all. She was overwhelmed and had all the items she inherited hidden away in a storage unit. However, she could no longer afford the monthly storage costs and needed to move everything out by the end of the month. She had literally just walked over to her neighbor's house to ask for his help in moving the items when I pulled up.

After I heard this story and learned of this practical need, I could not contain my excitement.

"This is a divine meeting, Wendy!" I exclaimed. "Let's schedule a moving day!" Once again, it's amazing she did not call the police on me, especially after curiosity got the best out of me when I tried "qualifying her" as a widow by at one point, awkwardly asking, "So are you the only one in the house?" Looking back, this was a poor question to ask. Like I said, there were a lot of things that could have gone awry here—but I was becoming a provider one messy step at a time.

Next, I did what was the natural next step to solidify our friendship. We took a selfie together and hugged. We had our person in need.

That is what happens when you start engaging your provider muscle. You notice opportunities. You create opportunities. You bless and protect in ways you never expected.

Following Through

A few weeks later, a dozen or so guys showed up and helped Wendy on moving day. She was elated—and so was her neighbor who no longer had to be the one to move all her stuff! The day was nearly a perfect success. The only casualty was my phone. The screen cracked after falling off a ladder as I yet again wanted a picture to remember this moment. The casualty of my phone's screen reminded me how moving from selfish living to unselfish living can hurt sometimes. It costs us something to live for others. Most of the time it costs us our comfort. It's comfortable living for yourself, but that does not mean that is life-giving. I didn't care about the phone. In fact, I kept the crack for months as a reminder of the cost of becoming a provider.

At the end of moving day Wendy and I were standing outside her house. Her stuff was out of storage and the guys had done an excellent job serving her well. Wendy looked at me and, with tears forming in her eyes, said, "You don't know how much this blessed me. Keep doing what you are doing; even if it doesn't always work out, you will be blessed."

Her remarks struck me so deeply that I immediately transcribed them on my phone when I got into my car. If I'd never taken a risk, if I'd never stepped outside of my needs, we would have never met Wendy and witnessed how we can bless others and how the Bless and Protect Matrix and Provider Wheel can go from theory to practice.

24

A SECOND DEATH

I USED TO RUN AWAY FROM SUFFERING. NOW I KNOW WE ARE
CALLED TO GO THROUGH SUFFERING.

There are some wonderful moments and payoffs when you become a provider. Helping Wendy was a life-giving experience and a textbook example in many ways. However the call to become a provider may expose you to new challenges you never thought you could overcome. Challenges that cause much more damage than a cracked phone.

I know what it means to feel totally spent, only to be asked for more. To feel pain, only to endure a new injury before you have had time to fully heal.

Giving until it hurts forces you to either give up or to rely on God. We can burn out or we can lie down in green pastures as Psalms 23 tells us and receive the blessing and protection from our heavenly Shepherd to keep providing for others. I was tested between giving up or getting refueled when I received another terrible phone call.

"There has been a fire."

This time it was Mom on the line delivering the news. It had been just over three months since Pop's death, and now this. The Lodge was in flames.

Pop spent the majority of his retirement days at what we called "the Lodge," a beautiful rural property that had been in the family since my grandfather. Pop loved to hunt and camp there. He built a house on the property and Mom quickly discovered he preferred that location over their home together in town. After his death we kept the Lodge largely untouched. Everything in it represented Pop. From the mounted animal heads on the walls to his woodworking shop in the basement, it all embodied his passions and personality. Here was where Pop had breathed his final breath. Simply put, the house allowed us to feel connected with Pop in the wake of his loss. And now it was gone.

I was stunned. I hurt for Mom again.

Mom had walked into the house to discover total devastation. Everything on the main living area charred. There was a hole burned through from the living room to the basement.

There would be more questions than answers.

Sadly, we would learn that this was not a natural or accidental fire. It was an arson case.

Questions rattled our brains for the coming days, weeks, and months. Who did this? What on earth was the motivation? How could we move on from this?

We knew someone had broken into the Lodge, our private sanctuary. As if this first offense wasn't enough damage, the perpetrator(s) attempted to burn it all down. They poured gasoline and started a fire in the middle of the living room with the intention of destroying the house.

The local fire department and sheriff's office got involved. After arson was confirmed, the state police assigned an investigator. Our insurance company hired a senior fire investigator to review the case as well. This was serious.

No one had answers but everyone agreed on one thing: this was a malicious arson attempt. The motivation was not theft, rather destroying the house. They left tools, firearms, even credit cards untouched. This frustrated the team of investigators and our family.

The investigators told us if the perpetrator(s) had left a window open or door cracked the house at all it would have burned to the ground. Instead, the house was so tightly sealed that the fire lost oxygen and went out, but not before total devastation inside.

This hurt on a number of levels. I remember telling my wife it felt like a second death. The house had been an unofficial memorial of Pop and his life, now it was a hard place to return, now forever damaged. The house represented memories and stored precious items that allowed us to hold on to our previous reality as a family. Now that was taken away from us.

Instead of being allowed to grieve the loss of Pop we were thrust into an investigation and insurance claim that left us battered and torn emotionally as a family.

Going to the property and seeing it blocked off with yellow criminal tape deepened the feeling of loss.

After I got the call from Mom, I once again packed up the family and drove to see her, not knowing what to do. I wanted to be there for her but felt lost all the while—too familiar of a feeling.

This time, on top of grief, there was anger. There was frustration. Hopelessness.

When I arrived at the Lodge, I paused before crossing the threshold which held so many memories. This was where I felt closest to Pop. It was a sacred place and it was now literally in ruins. The most significant physical reminder of Pop had been destroyed.

I had to hold my breath to protect myself from the fumes and gases of the smoldering house. I didn't want to face the destruction, but I knew I needed to. We had to take meticulous inventory of everything in the house, racking our brains to remember if anything was missing. We had to answer scrutinizing questions from investigators, trained to trip people up in their own words in case we were being deceitful. All of this was going on while we were in a daze, hardly believing we were living through yet another family loss. The arson expert kept asking the same questions and then it dawned on me—I was a suspect. Mom was a suspect. Our family was no longer protected at the Lodge; it was the focal point of a serious investigation.

I don't know what obstacles, difficult conversations, and hard places you are facing as you embark on your provider journey, but this is what I've learned: we need to return to the hard place in order to pass through tribulations. We are not called to naively avoid hardships, hoping for the best. Becoming a provider means we get to the other side by going through hardships.

There was nothing else to do other than move forward with all parties and work toward rebuilding. It would serve as a physical representation of the rebuilding that needed to happen in our lives after the loss of Pop.

You may find, as I did, that you were truly given a gift in tragedy. Before Pop passed I wasn't driven to provide. Now, even when I felt I had nothing to give, I knew I was providing by being willing to go through suffering rather than running away from it.

25

TIME TO BE EXPOSED

I USED TO THINK BEING EXPOSED WAS A NIGHTMARE. NOW I
KNOW BEING KNOWN IS A SWEET BLESSING.

The arson it made me reflect on the wonderful memories at the Lodge. Unfortunately the investigation fell short of any conclusive evidence, let alone convictions. We were left struggling to understand why this happened and how to rebuild.

As we rebuilt the Lodge, there was one specific memory at the house that stood out as most significant, head and shoulders above all others. It was the story weekend. I have a framed picture in my office from that weekend as a daily reminder of what I learned from Pop's example of showing weakness to his sons in order to build up our own strength and become providers.

———

February 2017

"Well," Pop said over the phone, "I guess it's time to expose myself."

I paused, waiting for Pop to continue. This comment came out of nowhere during what I thought was a routine Sunday evening call with Pop. What did he mean—"expose myself"?

"I'm all ears," I said as I sat down in my office chair ready to listen, now fully concentrating on his every word. This casual conversation had just shifted into something more, or so I thought.

Pop reset my expectations.

"Let's schedule time together at the house with John, so I don't have to repeat myself and you guys can be there together." In his own way, Pop was telling me he was ready to share his story, to be known. I had no idea what he meant by "exposing himself" but I now knew it was not going to happen during this call, rather it was a moment reserved for the Lodge.

I gripped the phone, disappointed that I was not going to hear more in the moment, but thrilled about the opportunity to learn more about Pop. I had never heard anything like this come out of his mouth before. With a combination of excitement and perplexity, I wondered what story Pop had to share. He had never even indicated there was anything to expose. I had just been thrown into a mystery plot and I was eager to hear more.

Pop, who never wanted to be a burden, continued, "It doesn't have to be soon, just a convenient time that works for everybody. Any time will work just fine."

I quickly jumped into action. "I'll talk with John and we will organize a time that works for everyone." I hung up the phone with Pop and immediately called John.

"So Pop wants to share his story with us."

"Ha, what?" my brother exclaimed.

"That's right, he just called out of the blue and said he wanted us both there and it's up to us to schedule a weekend."

March 2017

A couple weeks later my brother and I were driving in the car together to hear Pop's story. We had both packed up the wives and kids and driven out of state for this moment. While our families stayed in town with Mom, John and I soldiered on to meet

Pop at the Lodge. We couldn't decide how to prepare for the moment or what to bring to the occasion. We hedged our bets and bought a variety of processed foods just to ensure all boxes were checked. Pre-made grocery sushi, check. Bag of Cool Ranch Doritos, check. And finally, a six-pack of Coors beer. Disclaimer: these purchases were all made before my health coaching career.

As I hugged a turn on the tight rural roads heading into Floyd, Virginia I asked John, "What in the world do you think we are going to hear?"

"I have no idea!" John smiled back.

Neither one of us had been able to gather any more intel from Pop since his phone call. Even with all the ambiguity and uncertainty surrounding the day, we knew we were about to experience a special moment. Here is an excerpt from my journal the day before:

God, tomorrow is when John and I go to Floyd to hear Pop's story—or as he put it, 'time to expose my myself.' I really want this to be a private, intimate moment and ask that you help it to be a powerful, real conversation between the three of us and you. Thank you for organizing this moment and for ordaining it. May your will be done. May I bring an open spirit and presence to the day, ready to hear Pop's story and to love him and respect him. In your name, Amen!

John and I arrived at Pop's retirement lodge. Nestled away from civilization, it was our safe haven. Peaceful and quiet. We opened up a couple beers and sat down at the kitchen table ready. I intentionally did not bring any notebooks or anything to distract from the conversation. As my prayer indicated, I didn't want to "poke the bear." If Pop was in the mood to share, the last thing I wanted to do was to get in the way. I wanted to be in the moment and savor it. I didn't want to invade his privacy by asking him to speak loud enough to be recorded on my phone or to distract the conversation by taking notes. I simply sat down and was fully present.

The moment was finally here.

"Feel free to ask me any questions. It may help me remember more," Pop began. John and I sat at the kitchen counter, silent as Pop started to share his story. Over the next several hours, Pop shared more weaknesses and failures in his life than I had ever dreamed existed. I was on the edge of my seat in disbelief. Pop lived up to his initial description of "exposing himself." He genuinely wanted to be known and understood by his sons. It was an incredible moment to experience.

After he had shared what was on his heart, Pop suggested we go to dinner. This is where we took our last picture together that now hangs in my office. John and I were about to leave for the night to return to our wives back in town. I needed to ask Pop a final question before leaving.

"How much of this story can I share?" I knew our wives would ask us questions and I wanted to honor Pop's wishes and respect his privacy, which he valued so dearly. He laughed back at me.

"Well, you can share what you wish. I didn't want this story public when you kids were growing up, but I will just leave that decision to you now."

It is with that permission from the man himself and my mom's blessing to share with you a summary of Pop's story from prodigal son to a strong provider. This story models how anyone, at any point in their life, can become a provider.

26

POP'S STORY

I USED TO THINK I KNEW POP. NOW I KNOW HIS TRUE PROVIDER JOURNEY.

W hen Pop was twenty-four years old he was still living in his hometown, working for his well-respected father at the family furniture store. He was a restless soul who would go on long road trips in the summer and who still enjoyed hanging out with his high school friends who also mostly stayed in the area.

As he searched for meaning and pleasure, he discovered drugs and the lucrative business of selling marijuana in 1974. That's right—Pop, my father and model provider figure, was a drug dealer.

Although he lived in a small town, this was no small-time operation. Pop organized large substantial drug deals in Southwest Virginia. He enjoyed the freedom that came from having extra money and the thrill of living on the edge. What started out as small purchases for his house parties escalated quickly.

"He only had high-quality stuff," remarked one of his friends.

Pop's desire for travel and freedom paired well for growing business.

One of Pop's long-time friends remarked, "He was living pretty large. Spending money and all, [...] it was a pretty substantial operation. Not just buying and selling pot—this was an enterprise."

Eventually Pop was making trips to Arizona to get a trunk full of marijuana that was shipped in from Mexico. He would then transport it back to Virginia for distribution. Eventually his cross-state drug runs caught the attention of the FBI. The FBI's Drug Enforcement Agency had just been created in 1973 and they had received the backing of the president himself to prosecute and convict drug dealers harshly.

> On March 28, 1973, President Nixon submitted to Congress Reorganization Plan No. 2, saying, "This administration has declared an all-out global war on the drug menace." He urged the consolidation of all anti-drug forces "under a single unified command." Although the metaphors were military, there was at least a suggestion that the end was not victory but vigilance, and that the new organization was here to stay. It was named the Drug Enforcement Administration (DEA).[1]

Eventually Pop's trunk load deliveries escalated to tractor trailer loads of drugs and inevitably his name was brought up to the authorities. Some assume it was his drug-dealing partner, others believe an undercover cop discovered Pop's side hustle. What is certain is that there was a federal warrant out for Pop's arrest. Jail time was expected to be around five years for illegally purchasing and distributing marijuana across state lines.

When Pop heard that his name had been turned into the authorities he had a decision to make. Face the reality of his actions and take responsibility or …. not.

Pop chose to run. He became like the prodigal son from Jesus's parable in Luke 15. One day he was at the furniture store and the next no one heard from him. It was the beginning of a dark period in his life. Pop was officially on the run and off the grid in 1974.

For nearly five years, he was a fugitive.

Federal agents went as far west as Arizona and even into

Canada searching for him. They wanted to make a statement that drug dealing across state lines was a felony. Pop bounced from Virginia to Tennessee to North Carolina, down to Mexico, and eventually settled on a ranch in California. He took on aliases, trusting no one during this time. He would tell acquaintances he would meet on the run that he was going north and then head south. He needed to stay one step ahead of the authorities.

There were some close calls during his time on the run. One time a police helicopter located Pop's whereabouts in Arizona and searched up and down with a spotlight in the middle of the night. Another time Pop heard a "click" on his landline phone and knew it was bugged. He quickly ran out of the house, leaving a burning fire in the fireplace to escape the oncoming cops.

However, the best part of this story in my opinion is that he met Mom while on the run. Not only did he meet her during this harrowing time in his life, he met her under an alias!

I had always assumed Pop had lived a stereotypical life of working, having kids, and providing financially. Now I was grappling with how much he had changed through serious challenges and poor decisions before becoming that model provider. Also, I just could not get over the fact that Mom married Pop when the relationship started with a lie. I mean, what woman trusts a man using an alias, living out of a van, on the run from the law! Sometimes I just reflect on the miracle that I am alive today.

It was not all fun and adventures on the run. There were times of loneliness and uncertainty to push through. Then, there was a tragic loss.

While Pop was still on the run, his mother died of cancer.

Because of his selfish decisions, he was unable to bless and protect his own mom when she needed him most. Her youngest son was nowhere to be found during her final days and she was left wondering, "Where is my son?"

Fortunately, God was blessing and protecting Pop during this time. God spoke to Pop in a number of ways during this season of life, including orchestrating meeting Mom and a Christian pastor who both helped to inspire him to turn his life around. After the loss of his mother, hours of praying, and receiving counsel from a pastor, Pop decided it was time to turn himself in.

In one of the first steps of coming clean, Pop wrote a letter to Mom. They were casually dating at the time and he wanted to be known to her so he first told her the truth through a letter. He told her he was not Ken; his real name was Calvin and he was not a rancher, but rather a fugitive on the run. He informed her that he was turning himself in later that week. It was 1979. It was Pop's turning point in his life.

Standing before a judge in West Virginia with his father, brother, sister, and pastor from California standing by his side, Pop waited for the judge's verdict.

Pop had come back to answer to his mistakes. He told the judge that he was not there to turn anyone in, just himself, and he was prepared to face the consequences for his actions. Pop's faith had grown during this time and he was confident that God's will would be done.

The judge ended up convicting Pop of a felony, but miraculously waived all jail time. Pop was restored to society and was given another chance. By the end of 1979 Pop was back at the furniture store with his father, a newly convicted man. Even more miraculously, Mom kept in touch with Pop over the years and they married in 1982. Pop even had his felony pardoned and expunged from his record. He was restored back to full citizenship.

On course to throw his life away, Pop did a 180-degree turn and took responsibility for his biggest mistakes in a way that hardly any man would. And he was not ashamed. It highlights the extent to which he worked on developing a life of personal integrity.

Are you familiar with the parable Jesus tells of the prodigal son in Luke 15? One of the sons of a wealthy father asks his father for his inheritance early and runs off. He lives wildly, squandering his life for awhile before returning to his father in desperation and begging forgiveness. His father (representing our heavenly Father) runs to greet him and lavishes him with forgiveness, restoration, and a party in his honor. He is restored to not only his role as a son, but also full honor.

This was my father's story.

Writing this summary of Pop's prodigal son journey is a reminder that despite our baggage, we *all* can become providers. We can all be the father in the Prodigal Son story, blessing and protecting others.

I am so thankful to have heard it directly from Pop. Just two weeks later, he died.

He shared his life as a cautionary tale to protect us from the same path. I finally knew my father. Hearing his story allowed me to connect with him, appreciate him, and then pass through the anger stage of grieving more quickly because of the gift of the story weekend.

Why did he wait so long to share with us? I believe it was all God's timing. The better question might be, *Why did he decide to share his story at all?* Perhaps Pop was motivated to share his story so that we didn't hear it from someone else. He lamented that day during the story weekend at the lodge how he couldn't learn anything new about his father or grandparents who were all gone. This seemed to motivate him to share with us in person while he still could. He had no idea he only had days to live, or perhaps he sensed the end was near. I believe it was all God's timing.

The power of being known and sharing our story became real to me that day with Pop and my brother. I had never felt so close to my father. In fact, in my the last journal entry before Pop passed away I wrote:

I spoke with Pop for the first time since last weekend's story and it was a genuine, natural flowing conversation. What a gift.

We never know how much longer we have to share our story. No one expected Pop's heart attack or even considered that his days were so limited. Having that weekend helped me quickly progress past the anger grieving stage after his death. How could I be angry? I was given a gift. He opened up his home and heart, in his own way. Pop wasn't a frilly, hospitable person. He wasn't the kind to grab a microphone or pen his testimony for the world to be hear. But he wanted his family to know him—the real him. We sat on the deck overlooking his property and shared beers. We went out to eat after this at the "nice" restaurant in the rural town. It was all classic Pop. He didn't tell his story in a linear fashion, he didn't use the cleanest language, and he repeated himself and left out important details for us to prompt him. But he shared. It was a moment I will always remember. It is a moment I try to replicate in each fellowship class to the best of my ability. He provided by sharing his story and being known. We can do the same for others.

Afraid you've messed up too much to provide? Feel stuck in that selfish quadrant? Remember that even the farthest prodigal can become a strong provider if you put your life in God's hands. Know that it will be painful. It will require sacrifice.

You must give until it hurts. My father put his very life in God's hands by turning himself into the police after years of being on the run. It was rough—they actually tackled him into submission when he showed up at the station and gave them his name! It wasn't easy, but he spent the rest of his life choosing to bless and protect others. I'm sure Pop struggled with the temptation to ride off into the sunset alone and never face his past. He didn't do it perfectly, but he gave it all—down to the very story that defined him as a provider.

27

YOUR TURN

I don't care where you are on the Bless and Protect Matrix or how jagged your Provider Wheel may look today. If you have a desire to improve and are ready to be held account-able, you are ready to become a provider. As Stephen Covey once said, "The key to growth is to learn to make promises and keep them."[1] The first step is to keep the promise to yourself that you will do something about your desire to become a provider.

You can take the information in the book and run with it. That was my original idea. I was going on a solo soul-searching journey to try and discover how to become a provider. However, God planted that word *fellowship* in my head and I realized I would grow into a better provider if I did it in community. Fortu-nately I discovered the joy of blessing and protecting others through community.

We were designed for fellowship. My pastor defined fellow-ship as "the faithful and consistent act of sharing and doing life together with Jesus Christ at the center." I even learned that the word *fellowship* comes from the Greek word *koinonia,* meaning "having in common, partnership and participation together."[2]

Imagine the growth you can have by surrounding yourself with others trying to become providers based on a biblical world-view. Your chances of success will be much higher. In fact there was a powerful study into how relationships actually help us to change behaviors better than facts or fears.

Researchers wanted to try and figure out what makes people change. Their hypothesis was people change when faced with life-and-death odds. So they followed patients who were suffering from a deadly heart disease. Physicians told these patients they had to adjust their lifestyle and diet in order to live. This is literally life-or-death stuff! How many patients do you think changed out of nine? Probably seven or eight at least right? Nope. Only one out of nine are likely to make sustainable change. That is a sobering statistic. This study indicates that facts and fear do not motivate us.[3] This research and statistics made a lasting impact on my since Pop passed away from a related coronary heart disease. It also highlights how although we may have been told all the facts to do something positive in our life we may still not actually do them. Don't let the Provider Wheel be the next helpful resource to go unused in your life.

My desire is that you actually take action from this book. Commit to earnestly praying for people in your life. Demonstrate radical generosity to others. Your life will change forever. And there are many more fantastic ways of blessing and protecting others in your life.

So how can we be the one to change? Better yet, how can we help others become providers as well? It's all about relationships and is why the the CL Thomas Fellowship exists. From behavioral science research, psych concepts, and scientific studies there is a consistent theme around the need for relationships in order to help us make lasting changes in our lives.

Lasting change happens when we have new relationships which support us and gives us hope. CL Thomas Fellowship groups are led by a mentor or "provider coaches" who believe that each fellow can be a great provider. The mentor facilitates monthly meetings and models a lifestyle commitment of becoming a provider. In addition, the fellowship offers a growing library of recorded interviews from experts in different areas of the Provider Wheel. We are building a community who all strive to help one another to become providers.

One of the most exciting new additions is that my wife is now leading the CL Thomas Fellowship for women. They take the same wheel and the same calling of blessing and protecting others through the unique gifts and callings that God has placed on their lives as women.

Whether or not you join a formal fellowship group I encourage you to start providing. Discover the joy of blessing and protecting others for yourself. The heart of being a provider and providing like Jesus is serving others, not yourself. It's not only a high bar, it's a pull-up bar. You may feel like you've mastered a certain provider characteristic trait. Just when you've got a grip around a concept, you realize there is more to do. You need to lift yourself higher in order to bless and protect others even more. This strength needs to come from an unrelenting belief and confidence that the great Shepherd, the Lord Jesus, is holding you up and over to get over that pull-up bar when you need a spotter.

As Oswald Chambers once reflected, "To say that 'prayer changes things' is not as close to the truth as saying, 'Prayer changes me and then I change things.'"[4] We need to get to know God through prayer, receive his guidance and use the blessings and protecting we received to *change things for others*. We need to become a provider for others when the moment is right and you see whom you are supposed to bless and protect.

EPILOGUE

I was once again wearing Pop's leather vest.

Similar to Pop's funeral reception I looked out into a room filled with friends, family, and mentors. Except tonight we were not just celebrating Pop's life, but his provider legacy. Tonight's event was a celebration dinner, commemorating the successful launch and completion of the first CL Thomas Fellowship class.

Sometimes you just need to throw a party in life. I wanted to celebrate the wins of life in the face of its harsh new realities. This dinner event would turn out to be one of the most special evenings of my life. I wanted to make the evening a memorable one, God would ensure it would be.

We had family members drive in from out of state to attend. We even had friends from abroad fly in for the dinner event. The men who just completed the fellowship were in attendance along with their wives. Several of my mentors were present. It was a room full of people who had poured into my life and also into the Fellowship. Most importantly, Mom was there.

We enjoyed dinner together and then I stood up. It was time to share how the year went and the tools we use to help us become providers.

I showed a testimonial video highlighting the first fellowship class and how their definition of "provider" had expanded. I then shared how we were scaling the fellowship beyond me and equipping other men to lead their own groups. It was exciting news. Then I announced this book project for the first time publicly. I read excerpts about Pop and how he provided and my struggle to understand how to provide like Pop. When I finished sharing all of these exciting updates I felt the night had been a grand success. However, the most powerful moment was still coming.

As people started to leave they thanked me for a great evening and congratulated me on the fellowship. It had been a special moment and I was starting to feel pretty good about all the planning I had done. Yet the night was not about me and my effort. Fortunately God showed this to me by directing my attention to Mom's table. I looked over from the front of the room, collecting my items from the podium and witnessed the men who had just completed the fellowship program get up in unison and walk over to Mom's table.

The guys introduced themselves one by one to Mom in a respectful, honoring fashion. I was immediately struck with the scene unfolding before my eyes as I witnessed these men become providers.

I proudly looked on as I saw one fellowship graduate after another hug Mom as she cried into their arms tears of joy, pain, and gratitude all wrapped into one. They had blessed and protected her. This moment represented all of the provider characteristics. This not only made my night but also Mom's and she sent me this message to honor the moment:

One of the most meaningful, special nights of my life. I will always enjoy the memory. It's just so incredible to see your vision alive and in a way that is so honoring to Pop. He was a very unique man and it is very rewarding to see his life have an impact on young men. What a great group of people gathered together tonight!

Become a provider; it's who we are called to be. We are all gifted in a unique way to bless and protect one another. A provider gives sacrificially. It will hurt and stretch you beyond what you think is possible. Then you will experience the blessing and promise that Psalm 23 provides: "The Lord is my shepherd, I shall not want." You will be provided for over and over again so that you can do the same to those in your spheres of influence.

I'm committed to this work for life. I have no idea how small or large God wants this provider movement to go and what role the fellowship will have in it. I consider myself lucky and blessed to have had Pop as a father who allowed me to know my heavenly Father, Jesus.

I'm still trying to figure out how to provide like Pop. I am honored to be on this journey with you all in becoming the provider God wants us all to be.

Enjoy blessing and protecting others.

ACKNOWLEDGMENTS

Pop's unexpected death introduced the most significant test of how my family lives with joy. I can honestly say this was both the hardest and the most rewarding period of my life. Writing this book forced me to clarify the lessons I learned and reminded me of all the people who breathed life into this project when I needed inspiration to carry on as a first-time author.

Mom, this book is dedicated to you for a reason. Thank you for your prayers; they have been powerful and effective in my life and I continue to be blessed by you.

To my lovely lady, my wife, Amy. I have had a front row seat in witnessing strength that I never knew existed. You allowed me space to grieve and the freedom to dream. Thank you for choosing me.

To my brother, John. A man whom I respect and with whom I can be fully known. Thank you for your support and encouragement. Pop would be so proud of how you serve your family selflessly.

Writing a book about the story of losing your father is a challenging process. I'm forever indebted to my sister-in-law and editor, Sophie, who guided me from start to finish with professionalism and empathy.

To Sister Amie. My love is unconditional.

To Tim Oakley and our men's group. God placed you all in my life to prepare a solid foundation for the challenges I endured after our group ended. I respect and love you.

To the extended Thomas Family. You held our family up when we needed a lift. From prayers we heard in person to all the silent ones I know you whispered in your own quiet times with the Lord. You have served as God's hands and feet for our family in practical ways since Pop's passing. Thank you dearly.

To the men of Dayspring Park. Over the past 25 years we have literally grown up together through middle school, playing basketball, and now as we continue to compete in our fantasy football league. I hope I beat you all. Thank you for your support.

To Pop's friends. Thank you for sharing stories of his life escapades. I know you would not want to be named publicly—especially for harboring a fugitive! You demonstrated loyalty and love through thick and thin.

To the men of F3 Churham who push me every week to improve my fitness, fellowship, and faith. Thank you for strengthening and challenging me.

Pastor Reggie & Bomi. Your friendship, mentorship, and support has been a blessing for over a decade. Thank you for serving as advisors from the beginning of our nonprofit work together.

To all the people who support the CL Thomas Fellowship; from the men who trust me to guide them along their personal provider journey to my mentors who pour into the program. Reaching between North Carolina and Ireland, you are all making a real difference!

Finally, to my daughters. Thank you for your motivation to become a better provider and for all the "help" when I was writing by sitting on my lap and drawing next to me.

Thank you all.

All proceeds from the sale of this book go directly to The CL Thomas Fellowship to equip people on their provider journey.

NOTES

2. The Gift of Becoming a Provider

1. "Provide", *Merriam-Webster*, accessed September 9th, 2019, https://www.merriam-webster.com/dictionary/provide
2. Psalms 36:5-8, Holy Bible, AMP

4. Pop's Final Letter

1. Acts 20:25, 32-37, Holy Bible, NIV
2. Generous Giving Media, "Tim Keller - The Gospel, Grace, and Giving," https://generousgiving.org/media/videos/tim-keller-the-gospel-grace-and-giving

7. Breakdown

1. Miller, James. *Winter Grief, Summer Grace.* Minneapolis: Augsburg Fortress: 1995.

8. Psalm 23

1. Psalms 23, Holy Bible, NKJV
2. Pfeiffer, Charles, ed.*The Wycliffe Bible Commentary.* Chicago: R.R. Donnelley & Sons Company, 1968
3. Ibid, emphasis mine.

12. What Am I Doing with My Life?

1. Ephesians 6:13,16, Holy Bible, NIV

14. The Hardest Part

1. Awaken the Greatness Within. "40 Inspirational David Goggins Quotes On Success." *Awaken The Greatness Within.* Accessed July 19th, 2019. https://www.awakenthegreatnesswithin.com/40-inspirational-david-goggins-quotes-on-success/

17. What I Learned Through Washing the Dishes

1. C.S. Lewis, *The Four Loves, ch. 1* "Introduction" p 7. (San Francisco:HarperOne, 2017).

21. Who to Provide For?

1. Luke 10, Holy Bible, NIV

22. When to Provide?

1. Galatians 6:2-5, Holy Bible, NIV
2. Dr. Henry Cloud and Dr. John Townsend, *Boundaries,* (New York: Harper-Collins, 2017).
3. James 1:22-25, Holy Bible, The Message

23. Wendy

1. Check out https://f3nation.com/ for more information on a local chapter.
2. James 1:27, Holy Bible, NLT

26. Pop's Story

1. "Drug Enforcement Agency" *The Early Years,* accessed July 15, 2019, https://www.dea.gov/sites/default/files/2018-07/Early%20Years%20p%2012-29%20%281%29.pdf

27. Your Turn

1. Stephen Covey, *Principle-Centered Leadership,* (New York: Simon & Schuster, 1992).
2. Bomi Roberson, "FOLLOW ME: FELLOWSHIP," Kings Park International Church, last modified August 11th, 2019. https://kingspark.org/sermons?sapurl=LysxYzliL2xiL21pLytkZmI5cjdoP2JyYW5kaW5nPXRydWUmZW1iZW Q9dHJ1ZQ==
3. Alan Deutschman, *Change or Die,* (New York: HarperCollins, 2007).
4. Oswald Chambers, *My Utmost for His Highest,* August 28th, (Uhrichsville, OH: Barbour Publishing, 1963).

Made in the USA
Columbia, SC
24 September 2019